NEGOTIATING HIGHER DESIGN FEES

NEGOTIATING HIGHER DESIGN FEES

by Frank A. Stasiowski, AIA

WHITNEY LIBRARY OF DESIGN
an imprint of Watson-Guptill Publications/New York

*To Anita, Kristin, and Erik, who stand by me
continually and give of their time so that I may
devote more effort to the improvement of management
in the design professions.*

First published 1985 in New York by the Whitney Library of Design,
an imprint of Watson-Guptill Publications,
a division of Billboard Publications, Inc.,
1515 Broadway, New York, N.Y. 10036

Library of Congress Cataloging in Publication Data
Stasiowski, Frank
   Negotiating higher design fees.
   Bibliography: p.
   Includes index.
   1. Architects—United States—Fees. 2. Architectural
services marketing—United States. I. Title.
Na1996.S73   1985   720′.68′8   84-20988
ISBN 0-8230-7383-1
ISBN 0-8230-7391-2 Pbk.

Distributed in the United Kingdom by Phaidon Press Ltd., Littlegate
House, St. Ebbe's St., Oxford

Manufactured in U.S.A.

First Printing 1985
3 4 5 6 7/95 94 93 92 91

Acknowledgments

Special thanks must go to several people without whom this book would not have been possible. Each has played a part in shaping my negotiating experience, and many have contributed directly to this effort.

1. O. C. (Russ) Tirella, long-time friend and fellow professional who first taught our Professional Services Management Journal (PSMJ) seminar on negotiating in 1979 and whose original concepts formed the basis for many current techniques.

2. Susan Le Comte, who patiently transcribed the entire manuscript from dictation several times, making editing more effective.

3. Michael R. Hough, publisher of PSMJ and first person to print many of my negotiating ideas and articles.

4. Susan Davis, who put up with delay after delay, but whose editing talent is unparalleled and without whom this book would not be what it is.

5. Stephen A. Kliment, whose initial faith encouraged me to begin this third book in the first place and without whom it might never have been begun.

6. Anita, Kristin, and Erik, who gave up time with me to allow me to work on the book for over nine months.

7. Louis Marines, my first friend in this profession without whom I might never have pursued a career in the management of design firms.

Contents

Foreword

Frank Stasiowski presents a full menu of negotiating suggestions to design professionals as more and more the competition for significant projects intensifies. Stasiowski's approach to negotiations has a familiar ring to those of us who have read or heard his presentations on marketing professional services. The negotiation of a contract that provides sufficient fees and conditions to perform the required services is indeed a continuation of the process of securing design commissions. All readers may not agree totally with every suggestion proposed, as consultant-client chemistry is ever-variable. However, Stasiowski covers the subject thoroughly with enough examples and practical suggestions to make this book easy and interesting reading: For those professionals who feel that they know how to negotiate, the book will provide many additional issues to consider that could improve their contract position on key projects. For those who feel that they need help, they will certainly find it here.

After setting the stage by defining the types of negotiation, strategies, and methods of planning and shaping the negotiation session, Stasiowski launches into his free-wheeling optimistic style that carries the reader right along with him.

I think that this book should be read and discussed in design firms of all sizes and practice profiles. Perhaps the design profession still has a chance to guide its own destiny rather than continue on the long retreat that has characterized the buyers market in recent years.

David G. Sheffield
Principal
The Architects Collaborative Inc. (TAC)
Cambridge, MA

Getting Ready to Negotiate

Part 1

Before starting any negotiation it is critical to analyze how to negotiate to get what you want. In this part of the book you will learn how to prepare for the process by exploring various types of negotiations and strategies to use as part of an overall plan.

① Types of Negotiations

- What are the biggest problems faced by today's design firm negotiator?

- What has brought you to where you are today in negotiations?

- What types of negotiation environments can you expect to encounter when negotiating?

- Why are certain environments bad for negotiating?

- What obstacles prevent design professionals from acting in a more businesslike manner?

- What can you do to avoid losing during a telephone negotiation?

- Is there a difference when negotiating for a contract with owners versus other design professionals?

In today's competitive world of negotiating design fees, design professionals often "take it on the chin" because of their lack of experience at negotiating. There are five primary causes of this:

1. Lack of business experience. Because most designers enter the field for artistic or professional reasons, they are not as concerned about business and financial matters as they are about design. Often their concern for professional decisions jeopardizes their negotiating position.

2. Little or no negotiating experience. Unlike many sophisticated clients, design professionals do not take courses on negotiating and in many cases have had no actual experience at negotiating a contract prior to entering a negotiation session itself.

3. Market pressure. During the past few years, with the economy in flux, designers have felt severe economic pressure to take every job, no matter what the fee. This type of pressure has placed many design professionals in a weaker negotiating position.

4. Fee scales. Until the early 1970s, most designers worked on a standard published fee schedule. Established fee scales eliminated the need to negotiate at all. Thus, until recently, design professionals were never forced to learn or use negotiating skills. But today these skills are required to be effective.

5. Frankness. Because of the strong feeling of allegiance to the client and because the design professional always wants to give the client the best service possible, many designers are too open when negotiating. Honesty does not mean that you must "show your entire hand" to the client in the first stages of a negotiation. Unfortunately, design professionals cannot assume that those opposite them at the negotiating table will be as honest as they.

The purpose of this book is to improve the design professional's capabilities at negotiating design fees. Throughout my years of experience as a registered architect and as a manager of design contracts, I have observed and practiced many of these techniques with great success. Each chapter is intended to give you real, nuts-and-bolts techniques that you can put to use immediately to help you negotiate a "fairer" deal on your next contract.

What Is Negotiating?

It has been said that negotiating is an art that takes years of practice to perfect. For design professionals, negotiating is the art of achieving a fair and profitable fee for the performance of quality professional work. It is the art of compromising on issues of scope and price while maintaining standards of work quality. The results of effective negotiating are satisfied clients who will give you good references or want to work with you in the future and work worthy of publication.

Of course, everyone's definition of a "fair and profitable fee" is probably going to be different, especially the client with whom you negotiate today. Likewise, how to judge the "quality" of design work is always difficult. Because of these and many other ambiguities, the job of the design firm negotiator is to continue the selling effort started by marketing personnel of continuously demonstrating the benefits to the client.

Chapter 1 sets the stage for the entire book by giving you a description of the types of negotiations that are encountered most frequently in our profession. As you read this chapter, note that the type of negotiation you face will have a large bearing on the strategy you choose (see Chapter 2).

One-on-One Negotiations

One of the negotiating types most frequently encountered by design professionals is the one-on-one negotiation. Many clients simply call the design professional for a lunch appointment and begin a negotiation session without the design professional ever realizing that he/she is being asked to negotiate a contract for a future project. Typical of this type of "lunch quicky" environment is the situation in which a developer may ask you out to lunch and begin discussions on a potential new project. Before lunch is complete, you are certain to be asked what fee you would charge. Without having had time for thought or preparation, you have been placed in a poor negotiating position.

The primary characteristic of a one-on-one negotiation is that one of the parties is unprepared while the other is totally prepared. Thus a one-on-one negotiation puts one of the parties at a decided disadvantage. One-on-one negotiations are predominantly win/lose negotiations (see page 33 for a definition of win/lose) in which one of the parties comes out of the negotiation feeling very good while the other feels that he or she has lost. The negotiation session itself is generally short, that is, shorter than many of the other scenarios we will describe, and the final agreement will not be well thought out.

In a one-on-one negotiation, the best advice is not to make any commitments unless you are really prepared to do so. Take time to research each item being proposed to you, and never sign an agreement unless you thoroughly understand all aspects of it. Also, review your commitments with all your partners or associates to be certain that you have not overextended yourself in the process of being anxious to get another job.

Telephone Negotiations

The worst negotiating environment of all is a telephone negotiation. A telephone negotiation occurs whenever a client attempts to finalize your fee in a telephone conversation. It is truly the ultimate quicky. In a telephone negotiation, all things are working against the parties attempting to negotiate a fair agreement. Design professionals, in their eagerness to satisfy the client and to get a project, many times overcommit themselves in a telephone conversation. There are six primary reasons why telephone negotiations are risky:

❶ The initiative lies with the caller. In a telephone negotiation the most prepared individual is the one initiating the call. When the initiative lies with the caller, that individual has already set the stage to win by being totally prepared and by taking the first step.

❷ Evidence cannot be used. Because physical evidence such as the use of an outside financial statistic survey or your own documentation of financial figures cannot be used on the telephone, it is difficult to justify your negotiating position during a telephone negotiation. Likewise, your estimate of hours to be spent on a project or your justification for hourly rates cannot be shown visually to the other party.

3 Calls happen too quickly. No one likes to stay on the telephone for long periods of time. Thus, telephone negotiations tend to be the shortest negotiations of all. In an attempt to get off the phone, either party may make commitments that they do not fully intend to keep.

4 Telephone calls force premature decisions. When either party in a telephone negotiation demands a "yes" or "no" answer, there is more likelihood that such an answer will be given than in any other environment. Because of the desire to end the phone call, the designer usually has no time to research many significant points, such as how this project affects the firm's overall manpower schedule, or how the current workload of the assigned project manager will fit into the project. Without doing any research, the designer risks making a premature commitment. In many cases this hurts the design professional both financially and in his or her ability to perform quality work.

5 Details are often forgotten. Talking into a telephone while negotiating is unnatural. As a result, your mind is not thinking as clearly as when you are negotiating face to face. In addition, long pauses are difficult to maintain and taking breaks to analyze proposals with your partners is impossible. Because telephone negotiations move rapidly, either party is likely to forget significant items that should be part of the negotiation. For instance, you may never discuss how you will be compensated for changes in scope during the project. The problem of lack of attention to detail is especially true if you are at the receiving end of the phone call.

6 Numeric errors are common. Individuals cannot quote numbers as accurately on the telephone as they can in person. Because there is no visual evidence displayed, it is difficult to assure accuracy in numerical calculations during a phone negotiation. Design professionals should be cautious when negotiating on the telephone, whether or not they initiated the call. Cautiousness can only help to preserve and enhance a relationship with a potential client. There are seven things to do to avoid making a serious mistake in telephone negotiation:

❶ Have a prepared checklist of what you want. Chances are you will be aware of a telephone negotiation ahead of time. If not, anticipate typical issues that are most important to your firm and make a standard checklist that is always next to your phone. This checklist should cover the pertinent items that are important to your firm's success, such as minimal profit levels, definitions of your desired work quality, and expectations of client/designer relationships during the project. Also, specify contract type desired, billing format, and frequency.

❷ Listen, don't talk. Especially if you received the call, it is more important to listen exactly to what the other party is saying. By listening you may gather information that allows you to structure your position more adequately to achieve the optimum result.

❸ Postpone the call if you are likely to be interrupted. It makes no sense to enter into a telephone negotiation if your secretary will interrupt you every three minutes with a message or with another call. If you are likely to be interrupted for any reason whatsoever, ask the caller to postpone the negotiation to a time slot when you can devote your entire energy to the process of negotiating. This tactic also gives you time to prepare a written strategy if you have not already done so.

❹ Take explicit notes. Perhaps even consider tape recording the conversation. It is important that your notes be substantive, qualitative, and accurate. Do not wait until after your telephone call to make notes. Do so as you are negotiating with the other party. Write down the specific numbers and terms that are discussed. Ask for clarification if needed, and take as much time as necessary to record everything accurately.

5 Confirm agreements quickly in writing. Immediately after hanging up, put all agreements into writing and send a copy to the other party. Telephone conversations are quickly forgotten. Verbal agreements can be lost if they are not confirmed in writing. Take the time immediately after hanging up to commit your entire agreement to writing so that both parties can review it.

6 Delay saying "yes" or "no." Making absolute commitments during a telephone negotiation is one of the most dangerous strategies. Try not to commit yourself to absolute answers. Instead suggest "maybe" or "perhaps." Another technique to delay making a commitment is to use the excuse that you must check with your advisory board, partners, or associates.

7 Recommend a meeting to finalize the agreement. Whenever an agreement is made, there will no doubt be changes after it is reviewed. It is human nature to change even the best wording in an agreement each time it is reviewed. By recommending a meeting to finalize the telephone agreement you allow yourself the opportunity to review all aspects of that agreement again with the party who called. A review meeting should be established on neutral turf, and a preliminary written agreement should be forwarded to each party prior to the meeting so that all arguments can be made with adequate preparation. By having such a meeting you give yourself the opportunity to rethink verbal commitments and to make changes before "inking the deal."

Undoubtedly, telephone negotiations will be used more in the future as clients try to minimize the time spent in the negotiation process. Beware that telephone negotiations are one of the most dangerous types that exist. Do not fall into the trap of overcommiting too quickly in a telephone negotiation without following some of the rules outlined here.

Inter-professional Negotiations

The most common negotiation type faced by design professionals is an interprofessional negotiation between one design professional and another for subconsulting services on a project. Whether it be an interior designer who is hired by an architect, or a civil engineer who is hired by a structural engineer, the environment is similar. Characteristic of this type of negotiation is an awareness of the scope of the project by both design professionals as well as a familiarity with the project type.

One major determinant in this type of negotiation is the timing, that is, whether or not the owner contract has been signed. When the owner has already signed the contract with the primary design firm, that firm generally has an advantage in the negotiation over any subconsultant. This is because the subconsultants must face the critical fact that they could lose the job if the negotiation does not favor the results of the already signed prime agreement.

If the owner has not yet made a commitment to a design professional, the door is open for a joint venture negotiation between two design teams. In a joint venture, the circumstances of the negotiation are different from those in a prime-sub relationship. For instance, design professionals from various firms work as a team to formulate negotiating strategy prior to finalizing any agreement with the owner. In many cases a temporary legal entity is formed to act as a joint venture to do the project. Thus a joint venture negotiation environment provides the opportunity for a mutual relationship that is much more beneficial to both design firms than in a prime-sub relationship. Checklist 1-1 points out the characteristics of a prime-sub relationship and Checklist 1-2 lists the features of a joint venture negotiating setting.

The driving force in an interprofessional negotiating environment is generally the strong desire on the part of each design professional to maintain a harmonious relationship after the contract is signed. Because most design professionals must work with other firms on a continual basis, often the nature of the immedi-

● Checklist 1-1. Characteristics of a Prime-Sub Relationship

○ One professional dominates the other.

○ Billing is from sub through prime to the client.

○ Prime design firm is the main conduit of project data for the sub.

○ Sub is generally paid after receipt of funds by the prime design professional.

○ Prime handles most coordination of drawings for various subs.

○ Owner meets directly with subs only infrequently.

○ Owner has a negotiating advantage over subs since the sub must negotiate through another professional instead of face to face.

● Checklist 1-2. Characteristics of a Joint Venture Negotiating Environment

○ Client contract not yet signed with design team.

○ Both parties view themselves as partners in the negotiation.

○ Equality of access to the client by both design firms.

○ Openness to share financial data between design firms.

○ Direct billing by either party to the prime client.

○ Joint coordination of drawings or other project data.

○ Better communication of project goals.

● Checklist 1-3. Characteristics of a Group Negotiating Environment

○ Requires longer time to conduct the negotiation.

○ More likely results in a mutually beneficial agreement.

○ Allows for preparation time.

○ Allows for more than one individual from each side to participate in the negotiation.

○ Explores all terms and conditions in depth.

○ Results in a written agreement.

○ Provides a forum for both parties to become more knowledgeable about each other's strengths and weaknesses.

○ Provides a training ground for negotiators from either party.

ate negotiation is not as important as the relationship that must exist subsequent to one project. Therefore, design professionals may sacrifice negotiating points in the interest of the subsequent harmonious relationship.

Group Negotiations

The most common type of negotiating environment for design professionals is a group negotiation. Group negotiations generally occur whenever a design agreement is negotiated with a sophisticated client. In a group negotiation, more than one party is present for each side. A target date is set for the negotiation, and each side is given a period of days or weeks to prepare their case. Another characteristic of a group negotiation is a planned strategy. Both sides choose their desired outcome and strategize how to achieve that outcome through a series of negotiating techniques. The most typical group negotiations occur on major projects with federal government clients. Design teams are asked to prepare elaborate documentation, and each detail is examined and explored in great depth during negotiations.

Because of the predominance of a group negotiating environment, much of this book deals with its consequences. The primary opportunity that a group environment affords is that it is the most likely environment in which both parties can achieve a harmonious agreement. Group negotiating sessions generally take a longer amount of time and require more preparation and energy. This means that group negotiating is most costly. However, if the results are mutually beneficial, the long-term advantage of a group negotiation session can be substantial. Checklist 1-3 enumerates the characteristics of a group negotiating session as they exist in today's design firm environment.

From a marketing point of view, the group negotiation session allows a design professional the best opportunity to build a relationship with the client that can last for many projects. A client willing to participate in a group negotiation can be viewed as a client willing to invest time in making the project successful.

Government Negotiations

A government negotiating environment presents the most defined environment in existence today for design professionals. Especially in the case of negotiations with the federal government, there are specific rules and regulations that apply to conduct during negotiating sessions. In most cases, the government negotiating session can be viewed as a group session with all the concomitant characteristics of group sessions. However, there are some major differences in government negotiations that are not applicable in any other type of negotiating environment. These include the following factors:

1 In most cases, the government has already prepared its overall estimate and knows exactly what its boundaries are with regard to the negotiating session prior to selecting the design team.

2 Government regulations set limits on the amount of money that will be paid for any specific item under a design firm contract.

3 Government negotiators have a significant amount of experience in handling negotiating sessions with design firms.

4 The organizational structure of the government body with which you are negotiating in most cases separates those who negotiate the contract from those who actually perform the work on the project.

5 There is often a great deal of government paperwork to be done.

For design professionals, the most significant aspect of a government negotiation is that those who negotiate the contract in most cases will not carry it out or have not created it. Because of the organizational separation within government bodies, it is most difficult for design professionals to prepare for such a negotiation. Also because those who negotiate the contract for the government will not carry it out, they may not have a stake in many of the terms that are negotiated as part of the agreement. This separation, combined with the government regulations and fee limits, poses the most difficulty for unprepared design professionals.

Thus, the most significant step to take when facing a government negotiating environment is to completely understand all the rules and regulations that apply to that body of government with which you will negotiate the contract. This may mean researching the law and studying the regulations in great detail to be certain that you are completely familiar with them, or at least as conversant as those with whom you will negotiate. Do not make the same mistake that many professionals make by thinking that a government negotiating environment will be the same as any other environment. It will not. See Checklist 1-4 for the typical problems encountered in negotiations with the government.

Because most government negotiators take the perspective of protecting the taxpayer, another ingredient in the government negotiation that may not be found in other environments is that of concern over fairness. Government negotiators want to accommodate both the taxpayer and the design professional to achieve a project at a fair and reasonable expense. Many design professionals have told us that the fairest clients they have are federal government clients. On the other hand, some design professionals view government negotiators adversely because of their own unpreparedness or lack of knowledge of government regulations. Keep in mind that government negotiators are

---

● **Checklist 1-4. Typical Stumbling Blocks for Design Professionals in Government Negotiations**

○ No knowledge of applicable procurement regulations.
○ Lack of substantiation for desired fees and pricing.
○ Professional (full-time) government negotiators.
○ Desire to do "highest" quality of design work when client wants less.
○ No knowledge of client invoicing procedures.
○ Minimal time spent in preparing for a government negotiation.
○ Belief that "good work" automatically assures repeat work.
○ No procedure to document changes in scope.

"trying" to protect the public while meeting the needs of whatever agency they are working with. Unfortunately, in many cases this need for public protection prompts public exposure of the negotiation itself. This can be one of the most adverse effects of a government negotiating environment. In Chapter 14 we will discuss how to work within the rules and regulations of government negotiations to benefit your side as a design professional.

Foreign Negotiations

Negotiating design contracts with foreign clients is perhaps one of the greatest challenges to American design professionals. Because citizens of other countries are often taught to negotiate from the time they learn to speak, there are many accepted practices in other countries that are totally foreign to the United States negotiator. Never, for example, are initial price quotes the final price we pay for an item, unless we fail to exercise any negotiating talent whatsoever. All of us have heard stories of American tourists who are fascinated with such bargaining in countries like Mexico or Italy.

Often those with whom we bargain were taught as children that the United States is a "rich" country. These very people may become the design professional's clients with whom we must negotiate design contracts. Having been taught from childhood many techniques for improving their negotiating position, they can often outwit the American negotiator unless we recognize many of the traits that are common to a foreign negotiating environment. Some of those traits include:

❶ Foreign negotiators always leave themselves room to negotiate. Unlike many American counterparts, foreign negotiators always quote a higher price than they expect to receive for any item. By doing so they leave themselves room to negotiate so that when their price or scope is reduced it is perceived to be a victory for the opposing party.

❷ Patience is a strong trait of the foreign negotiator, especially in Asian countries. For instance, recall when the Vietnam War negotiations were being held in Paris that the Vietnamese contingent actually purchased residences in Paris and moved their entire families to France for the duration of the negotiation, anticipating a long and drawn out process. Correspondingly, the American negotiators rented hotel space for six weeks and never brought their families with them. In America we are conditioned to do things quickly and expect that a negotiation will proceed fully within a specified period of time. In foreign countries time has no bearing on a negotiation, and thus patience is a strong trait in foreign negotiators.

3 Foreign negotiators use emotion to their advantage. Recall how Nikita Khrushchev used his shoe to bang on the table in the United Nations to understand how foreign negotiators use emotion to their advantage. Unlike foreign negotiators, Americans tend to be reserved business people who want to cooperate and establish mutual relationships. The use of emotion by a foreign negotiator can often force a decision that is premature on the part of an American design professional. Unfortunately, understanding the emotions of a foreign negotiator is not an easy task and requires great study prior to the negotiating session.

4 Foreigners concede slowly. Rather than giving in on any item, a foreign negotiator concedes slowly. By conceding slowly, the negotiator has drawn out every aspect of that negotiating term and has forced the American counterpart to commit or to anticipate greater concessions than are necessary. Also, by conceding slowly, the foreign negotiator establishes a psychological advantage on all future terms by creating impatience in the opponent.

5 Foreigners always negotiate with limited authority. The issue of authority is often a misunderstood item when negotiating with foreign individuals. American design professionals often anticipate that those negotiating with us are at an equal level of authority in their organizations. In many cases this is not true. Many design firms learned when entering the Mideast during the 1960s that negotiating took several sessions and that most likely the final negotiation did not occur until after they had negotiated with several teams of "limited authority" negotiators. When negotiating with someone with limited authority, commitment is difficult to achieve. Many horror stories are told about design firms that are promised thousands of dollars to accomplish a specific task by someone who had no authority to commit the funds. By negotiating with limited authority, a foreign design client can always back out of an agreement by deferring to a higher authority for final judgment. Also, remember that most foreign countries respect very strict hierarchical rules, which means that you must achieve success at the lower levels before moving on to higher levels of authority.

6 Foreigners always ask for something after having given something up. Keeping score is a talent learned early by foreigners. Foreign negotiators never concede to two items in a row without having received something from those with whom they are negotiating. Knowing this allows an American design professional to structure a negotiating session so that the foreigner can be given something every time he or she concedes even if what they are given is minor.

Understanding the traits of foreign negotiators is a full-time job. Because each country is different and because each culture and social structure within a country is different, it is important prior to negotiating with any foreigner that you study exactly how they have learned to negotiate. Remember that Asians and Arabs negotiate differently than Europeans and vice versa. Prepare each member of your team for what they will face in a foreign negotiation.

Comparing Negotiating Environments

Although there are combinations of all negotiating environments, remember that the six negotiation settings described here are the predominant types. With a complete understanding of each environment, a design professional can prepare a strategy that allows the firm to position itself in the optimum situation for any particular negotiation. The impact of each negotiating environment is different and when combined can be catastrophic if you are unprepared. As an exercise, go back and review the last few contracts that you negotiated. Try to determine if the negotiating environment had an impact on how the negotiation was conducted and on the outcome. List for yourself things that you would have done differently had you been aware of the negotiating environment and its impact on the outcome. Checklist 1-5 summarizes some of the characteristics of each type of negotiating environment.

● **Checklist 1-5. Characteristics of Each Type of Negotiating Environment**

---

❶ **One-on-One**
- ○ Short time period
- ○ One party unprepared
- ○ Little data available on the project
- ○ Price becomes topic of discussion early
- ○ No time to check with partners or associates
- ○ Verbal agreements common

---

❷ **Telephone**
- ○ Short
- ○ Caller prepared while receiver unprepared
- ○ No visual evidence
- ○ No time to analyze terms
- ○ Verbal commitments made too easily
- ○ Interruptions common

---

❸ **Interprofessional**
- ○ Work goals common to both parties
- ○ Well-understood scope issues
- ○ Mutually understood agreements
- ○ Common organizational structures
- ○ Knowledge of working relationships

---

❹ Group

- ○ Takes long period of time
- ○ Planned negotiating logistics
- ○ Tactics and strategies thought out by both parties
- ○ Much project data
- ○ Many participants
- ○ Detailed analysis of scope and terms

❺ Government

- ○ Regulated
- ○ Planned in great detail
- ○ Subject to audit adjustments
- ○ Professional government negotiators
- ○ Controlled logistics
- ○ Substantive project cost data

❻ Foreign

- ○ Full of emotion
- ○ Strict adherence to hierarchical procedures
- ○ Language and custom differences
- ○ Verbal agreement held to
- ○ Much give and take
- ○ Significant patience by foreign negotiators
- ○ Ceremonial logistics

2 Choosing a Negotiating Strategy

- How many strategies are there to choose from?

- When should you choose a strategy?

- How does your choice of strategy have an impact on your negotiating session?

- What impact does your strategy have on the outcome of your negotiations?

- Does wanting repeat work mean that you must choose a certain strategy?

- What if you beat a client in a negotiation *and* want to keep the client?

B efore discussing any technique with regard to negotiating, it is important for a design professional to choose a strategy. Then the entire negotiating session can be planned around that. There are four basic negotiating strategies available:

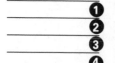

1. Win-win
2. Win-lose
3. Lose-win
4. Lose-lose

In this chapter we explore each negotiating strategy so that you will be totally aware of the impact of your choice on the negotiating techniques that will be discussed throughout the book. More than any other decision, your choice of a negotiating strategy has the greatest impact on the outcome of the negotiation. The wrong choice or resulting wrong techniques can and will work against you in every session. As you read this chapter, recall past negotiations and strategies that you have used and categorize them into any one of the four categories listed here.

A Historic Perspective

During the 1960s and 1970s a good negotiator was thought to be the individual who would win at all cost. Design negotiators were respected for their ability to have the client agree to every issue in the negotiation. Conversely, good client negotiators had the same perspective, and in many cases they were out "to get" the design professional without regard for mutual benefit or a long-term relationship.

In the latter part of the 1970s, a subtle but significant change began to occur as more negotiators became respected for their ability to achieve mutually satisfying agreements among the various parties. Thus the era of the "win-at-all-cost" negotiator came to a close in favor of the "win-win" negotiator. Because so many design professionals want to maintain long-term relationships with their clients and because clients want to develop working relationships with design professionals that avoid the necessity of repeat negotiation sessions, the win-win negotiator is in most favor today with the design professional and the client alike.

When choosing your strategy it is important to note this historic perspective. Many new clients and many design professionals still believe that it is most important to win at all costs. Thus it is important for your firm's negotiator to determine the perspective of your counterpart prior to beginning a negotiation. If you choose one strategy and your client chooses another, the result can be a lack of agreement or a mutually unsatisfactory agreement leading to a breakup of the relationship. With the cost of negotiating a design contract ever increasing, it is important to invest the time to research your client's strategy as you first plan the negotiation so that you do not end up making an incorrect choice. To do so, contact design firms that have worked with the client in the past. Fellow professionals can provide the best source of information on a client's negotiating posture. Another source of information is suppliers who provide services to the client, such as former contractors or material suppliers in the client's business.

The Impact of Poor Negotiating on Profit

When choosing a strategy, keep in mind that a poor negotiating session or a poor strategy choice may result in loss of revenue to your firm. For example, assuming that your firm is generating a profit of 10 percent per year on gross revenue, the impact of losing even $1 in revenue through a poor negotiating strategy is that you must generate 10 times as much in revenue on a future project to make up for that loss.

No matter how good your project management techniques or design capabilities, it is impossible to make up in the back room for the loss of revenue at the negotiating table. For this reason, note carefully each of the advantages and disadvantages of the four strategies before you begin planning for negotiating. Negotiating today is an expensive and necessary skill that is fast making the profession full of people who are capable and knowledgeable about each technique.

Ethics in Negotiating

Along with the choice of strategy, it is important to bear in mind your stance with regard to professional ethics in negotiating. There are three primary elements that should be discussed with your team prior to entering any negotiation session.

Truth. Truthfulness in negotiating is vital. It is important because from the beginning the development of a mutual relationship depends on building a trust between the parties. However, truthfulness does not imply that you must explain everything that you have in your strategy. Remember that you do not have to explain what you don't say. Thus, it may be important not to divulge immediately all aspects of your strategy, no matter how truthful you hope to be. Also, never bluff. You can be certain that the moment you bluff by threatening to walk out when you really don't want to, or by making an off-the-cuff threat, the client will call you on it.

For example, never threaten to delay a schedule or change team members unless either is absolutely necessary. Unfounded threats destroy trust, and once trust is broken, it is often impossible to reestablish. Thus, the only time to bluff is when you know that you will carry out the consequences.

Confidentiality. No matter what happens in any negotiating session, and no matter what strategy you choose for a negotiation, it is critically important that all aspects of the negotiation remain confidential. There is nothing worse than for a client to find out that what they have divulged to you through the negotiating process is then passed on to other design professionals for their use. Breaking confidentiality is tantamount to breaking the relationship that you have developed through your hard work in a negotiating session.

Thus, the cardinal rule of all negotiating is to respect confidentiality and never divulge even the slightest term that you have successfully negotiated. For example, do not even mention items like project schedule or team members used if you are called as a reference. Instead, defer any specific questions back to your client to answer.

Ruthlessness. There is no place in negotiating for ruthlessness. By being ruthless you only lose credibility as a design professional, you lose clients, and you start off on the wrong foot in any negotiating session. Remember that during the 1950s, 1960s, and 1970s the individual who was able to win at all cost was respected, but during the 1980s and beyond that individual will no longer be respected for using tactics that are perceived as ruthless.

As you choose any of the four strategies in planning for your negotiating environment, discuss and develop a position with regard to each of the above ethical issues. Remember that even if a client chooses to use tactics that you consider to be unethical, you do not have to follow suit. You should walk out on clients who ask you to consider any form of kickbacks or who ask you to compromise the work of others to save money.

Win-Win Strategies

Choosing a win-win negotiating strategy is the most advantageous, from a marketing perspective, for all design professionals. A win-win strategy is defined as a negotiating environment in which both parties believe they have won the negotiation at its conclusion. A win-win strategy encourages mutuality, which in turn fosters a long-term relationship. Since most design professionals want to keep clients longer than one project, it is important that the win-win strategy be completely understood when choosing it.

A win-win strategy is characterized by several distinct features, which Checklist 2-1 outlines.

One of the biggest problems identified in poor negotiations is the lack of a total understanding of the scope of work by either party in the negotiation. Because of the time-consuming and give-and-take nature of a win-win strategy, one of the most significant benefits is a complete understanding of the scope

○ Requires substantial preparation, with in-depth analysis of the client's potential negotiating strategy.

○ Demands the selection of the right team members for the negotiating team.

○ Takes longer time to accomplish at the negotiating table than any other negotiating strategy.

○ Is more costly than any other negotiating strategy because of planning time and advance expenditures.

○ Promotes mutuality between the client and the design professional.

○ Allows a trusting relationship to develop between the client and the design professional.

○ Is most beneficial for the outcome of a specific project because both parties want to perform well due to the results of the negotiation.

○ Requires that substantial data and information be collected before initiating negotiations.

○ Results in a beneficial, well-written agreement.

of work by both parties to the contract. When choosing this strategy, therefore, anticipate a long discussion on the issue of scope. Subsequently anticipate an equally long discussion on the subject of schedule and budget required to perform the scope. By choosing a win-win strategy and by pursuing the direction of an intense discussion of scope, the project can only benefit. Thus, prior to starting your negotiation, you have started on the first step toward an effective project and toward building a long relationship with a client. This strategy is most effective when dealing with a brand new client who is unsophisticated in the design marketplace.

Design professionals, such as interior designers or architects who deal with many unsophisticated clients, find that choosing a win-win strategy requires a more substantive investment of their time up front to educate their client, but this educational process leads to better contracts and to a better understanding of the entire scope of the work.

Win-Lose Strategies

Choosing a "win-lose" strategy in which you are the winner and the client is the loser usually means you will have a short working relationship with the client. Win-lose strategies are defined as "take it or leave it" in posture. A win-lose strategy (or, conversely, a lose-win strategy, which we discuss later) is for one-time projects only. For instance, if you know that a client has only one project and will never do another project and if you also know that the client has chosen a win-lose strategy himself, your best choice would be a win-lose strategy. The characteristics of a win-lose strategy are significantly different than those of a win-win strategy. A win-lose strategy usually requires a shorter negotiation with much more succinct negotiating tactics. Checklist 2-2 contains a list of such characteristics.

The most common reason for choosing a win-lose strategy is that you have discovered that the client has chosen one also. During the 1960s and 1970s, the win-lose strategy was the most predominant among all negotiators. Recall that to be an effective and respected negotiator in those days meant that you could

● **Checklist 2-2. Characteristics of a Win-Lose Strategy**

○ Takes a short time period for the negotiation.

○ Requires an autocratic negotiator to lead the winning team.

○ Requires substantial data and powerful information to overcome the obstacles of the client.

○ Results in a competitive instead of cooperative relationship with the client from the start.

○ Can hurt the outcome of the project being negotiated.

○ Results in a shorter written agreement.

○ Results in more change orders on the project.

○ Could have unfavorable long-term outcome due to the competitive nature of the relationship with the client.

defeat your client. There was no emphasis on building a mutually beneficial relationship. Today many small design firms take the position of choosing a win-lose strategy simply because they are not aware of the damage that it may do to them in the long run.

Prior to choosing your strategy, understand each of the characteristics in the checklists in this chapter. Then make a decision on the basis of the long-term benefit to your firm. A win-lose strategy would suggest that you use one of the negotiating environments that favors a shorter negotiating time than one requiring a longer time. This puts your client at a disadvantage, thus helping you win at the expense of the client.

Lose-Win Strategies

Although it would seem unlikely that you would choose a lose-win strategy, which means that you lose and the client wins, there are circumstances under which you might choose this strategy. For instance, if you are entering a new marketplace and desire to "make a mark" by doing a project at less than its value to your firm, you might choose to negotiate yourself into an unfavorable financial position. By giving the client a significant negotiating advantage, you hope it will influence them to choose to retain your firm in the future. Be cautious, however, because once you establish a price structure with a client, you may not be able to escalate it on a future project. A lose-win strategy should only be chosen when you know that you will lose and when you have decided that doing so is going to help the long-term goals of the firm.

One caution in negotiating a lose-win strategy: Set a bottom limit for the amount or terms that you are willing to lose. Set a walk-out price for each item of scope, and know when it is time to stop losing. Without a walk-out price for each item of scope, you may lose more than you have bargained for and end up not only with a losing project but also by losing the client. This is possible under the following conditions: If you take on a project that you lose at the negotiating table, you may be forced to cut corners. Doing so could jeopardize the client relationship because the client may feel cheated when you have to cut back on services in order to minimize your loss.

If you discover that you are in a lose-win situation that you had not planned, the best strategy is to lengthen the session by exploring every term in great detail. Stress give and take and caucus frequently to review the impact of each item. Only by stretching out the negotiation to allow for more trading do you stand to achieve a mutually beneficial agreement.

Lose-Lose Strategies

Under a lose-lose strategy, both parties lose on price or terms in the negotiation. It would appear that both parties have nothing to gain. However, a lose-lose strategy can have the benefit of giving mutuality to each of the partners in the loss. A good example of how this mutuality can be beneficial is when a design professional such as an architect and a subconsultant such as a mechanical engineer, with whom the architect is negotiating a fee, each end up taking lower fees to satisfy a client with a view toward establishing a long-term relationship with that client. Although both design professionals have "lost," they will probably get together to achieve the best results for the project so that the long-term relationship with the client can be beneficial. Under a lose-lose strategy, it is most important that both parties understand that the other has also lost. This may take special effort on your part when choosing the strategy. For instance, you may have to negotiate within your own firm for permission to lose money on a project so that long-term goals may be achieved. Be certain to include it in your planning. The choice of a lose-lose strategy should only be considered when a win-win is not attainable and when a long-term relationship with the client is important.

Choosing the Right Strategy

On the basis of long-term client relationships we would rate the four strategies as follows:

1. Best: win-win
2. Second best: lose-lose
3. Third best: win-lose
4. Fourth best: lose-win

Observation and experience show that the best strategy for a design professional is a win-win strategy. The most important thing to remember about choosing a strategy is that the choice should be yours. If a strategy is not chosen before you enter a negotiation, you may have no idea where you are going in the negotiation and you may be bewildered by the skill and tactics of your opposition. With so much competition in the marketplace today, it is important to retain good clients. Investing the time at the beginning of a negotiation is a sure way to start building a long-term relationship.

Prior to beginning any planning for an effective negotiating session, it is important to choose the strategy around which to build your tactics. As we have already described, there are four strategies available to you. Each strategy brings with it a set of characteristics that can be brought to bear by those in the negotiation.

Make sure you understand the implication of each characteristic of a strategy prior to beginning the planning for a design contract negotiation so that you are not surprised when the competition uses tactics associated with any one of the strategies listed. Whenever two parties in a negotiation use different strategies, most likely a win-lose or lose-win situation will result. Different strategies promote competition instead of cooperation.

If you have no strategy, the negotiating session itself will have no direction. Thus, all tactics chosen will be random and will result in a haphazard negotiation. Discuss each strategy in your firm and determine the appropriate direction for the project, the client, and the long-term goals of your practice. Don't simply let a strategy happen; choose it yourself.

3 Planning for Your Negotiating Session

- Why is planning important to negotiating?

- What impact do your firm's goals have on a single negotiation?

- Who should be involved in a negotiation?

- How do you collect data on your client's negotiating team?

- How much time should you spend planning?

- What should you bring to a negotiation session?

- When and how should you arrive?

- What is the significance of a walk-out position on a negotiating agenda?

Having chosen a negotiating strategy, it is now important to formulate a detailed plan of how to research all information necessary to conduct your negotiation, how you will establish the meeting environment, who will be part of the negotiation, and how you will conduct it.

Because the firm has just spent so much energy acquiring the project, there is often much resistance to spending more money in planning for the negotiation. However, more money can be won or lost at the negotiating session than can be made up in profit later on in the project. Thus, the importance of negotiating is equal to the importance of selling and marketing the project in the first place. Having a plan for the negotiation process is a vital element to its success.

Firmwide Goals

Prior to establishing a plan for a specific negotiation, it is important that each of the negotiators on the team understand the firm's goals in general. Long-range planning efforts by the firm should be shared with those who negotiate contracts so that negotiation sessions can take on the flavor and direction desired by the firm's partners. Without an understanding of where the firm wants to go, those in the role of the negotiator may contradict many of the basic tenets of the organization. Some of the firmwide questions that should be clear to those planning a negotiation session include:

❶ What is the profit goal of the firm for the year?
❷ What new markets does the firm want to enter?
❸ Who does the firm view as its competition in any new or mature markets?
❹ How much is the firm willing to invest in up-front fees to enter a new market?
❺ What is the firm's general policy with regard to design quality?
❻ Does the firm hope to have a high number of repeat clients or very profitable one-time clients?
❼ Is there a firmwide budget for the negotiating effort?

To this list add your own firmwide, goal-oriented questions. Remember that it is important for everyone in the firm to understand the direction that the firm wishes to take prior to entering into negotiations with any single client.

If you wish to conduct a discussion of firmwide goals with your executive officers or partners, consult Checklist 3-1, Strategy Planning Questions. Note that these questions cover a wide variety of topics, but a significant discussion can be centered around their use.

● **Checklist 3-1. Strategy Planning Questions**

Strategic Issues That Should Be Clear to Those Who Negotiate for Your Firm

○ What is your definition of growth?

○ How does your form of organization have an impact on growth?

○ Form a mental picture of what the practice should be like in three years.

○ What effect does the ownership transition plan have on growth?

○ What role will you play in your visionary practice?

○ What talent will you need that is not now present in the firm?

○ Why is growth important?

○ What impact does the management of time have on growth?

○ List three external factors that can help you grow, and then three that will hinder growth.

○ Define change.

○ How do you implement change?

○ What conflicts do you perceive between your visionary firm and the present situation?

○ What can you do to resolve the conflicts?

○ How do your clients perceive the firm?

○ Is their perception in line with goals for your visionary firm?

○ Crystallize your thoughts into a one-statement strategic goal for the firm in specific terms.

Marketing Issues to Consider before Negotiating

○ What are the three primary strengths of the firm?

○ Do your clients perceive these as your strengths?

○ Why do you call them strengths?

○ List three types of work in which the firm's strengths can be maximized.

○ List three more peripheral markets that you are not now serving but that could be entered using your strengths.

○ What kind of work should the firm do in order of priority?

○ What geographic area should be covered?

○ Define marketing.

○ Define selling.

○ What is the difference between marketing and selling?

○ What image does your firm project? How do you know?

○ What image will your visionary firm project?

○ How do the images differ?

○ Is there a project too large for the firm? Too small? Why?

○ Do you like to sell? List why/why not.

○ Do you have fear of sales' failure?

○ Write a specific marketing goal statement for the firm.

Financial Issues Affecting Your Negotiating Posture

○ Define profit.

○ How much money should you earn?

○ How much gross income will your visionary firm earn?

○ How does this compare with today's earnings?

○ Where will additional fees come from?

○ How much investment will it take to grow?

○ Are your sources of borrowing sufficient to fund the growth?

○ What is your profit goal for next year?

○ How does your profit goal tie in with your personal goal for income?

○ Do you want to communicate the financial status of the firm to the staff?

○ Should all owners have complete access to all financial data?

○ How much capital do you want to invest in the operations of the firm?

○ Is return of your investment important to you, and if so, how should it be measured—in terms of dollars and cents or in terms of your other goals?

○ List three financial factors affecting growth.

○ What control do you have over each factor?

○ What impact does the economy have on your finances?

○ List three things you can do today to improve the finances of the firm.

○ How can you enlist the help of the entire staff to improve profit?

Personnel Issues Affecting Your Negotiating Posture

○ Define motivation.

○ Define communication.

○ How do you communicate with your staff?

○ How does the staff perceive you? How do you know?

○ List 10 traits you look for in any person you hire. Rank them from 1 to 10 in importance.

○ Identify specific roles needed in your visionary firm that are not now present.

○ What is the goal of your recruiting effort?

○ List all benefit programs you now provide for your staff.

○ Next to each benefit, list how it affects your profit and how it helps you get more work.

○ How do your benefits compare with those offered by other architectural/engineering (A/E) firms? To other professional firms?

○ How does human resources planning affect market and financial planning?

The importance of firmwide goal setting cannot be overestimated. Without a direction, the firm can go astray. Likewise, without a direction a negotiation session can go in any direction.

After choosing your strategy for negotiating and studying the firm's goals, it is now time to begin planning your actual negotiating session for a specific project contract. You will need a written plan that can help a negotiator select an appropriate strategy.

Selecting the Team

One of the most critical decisions in planning for your negotiation is to decide how many people and who should go to the session. There are no general rules or guidelines with which to answer this question easily. However, there are many specific circumstances that can be discussed to assist you in choosing the right number of people and the right talent to be involved.

The more people in a negotiating session, the more difficult the planning becomes. Thus, put as few people as possible on a negotiating team. In general, no fewer than two and no more than three people are optimum for negotiating. A one-person negotiation is difficult because while that one person is talking there is no one available to listen to and assess the impact of the presentation.

In addition, it is difficult to caucus when you only have one person in a negotiating session. With two or more individuals, anyone can ask for a caucus or coffeebreak to discuss an item being negotiated. With any more than three people in a negotiating session, the complexity of planning increases exponentially with the number of people added. For example, to plan a negotiating session for four people is 16 times more difficult than to plan for three people. It is important that everyone in the negotiation have a role, even if that role is to be the silent partner with all the authority. It is not valid for anyone to go to a negotiation session simply to listen. A silent person who has no role will prompt the other party to distrust your organization.

When choosing the specific individuals to attend the negotiating session, it is not important to choose individuals by title. It is more important to choose them by the role that they play in the negotiation. Although there are several roles to be covered, you should still have no more than three people on the team if possible.

Scope of Services. It is critical that someone be on the negotiation team who can address all aspects of the scope of services being proposed. Generally, this individual is the project manager. However, in many instances there are engineers, architects, or interior designers who are more knowledgeable about the specific scope of a project than the project manager. In such cases, those individuals should be part of the negotiating team and their role should be to deal in detail with the scope of the project.

Financial Commitment. The second role that must be covered by a negotiating team is the ability to commit the firm financially on any issue within the negotiation. In many cases one individual who is the project manager or partner can commit the firm financially. However, with larger firms it may be necessary for the treasurer, business manager, or financial manager to be part of the team to assure that the client receives adequate information on financial questions. Having someone with financial capability on your team, as well as someone with the authority to commit the firm financially, gives you power in the negotiation to understand exactly what the client is saying when they ask for a reduction in a multiplier, a percentage point difference in a fee, or a different price structure for reimbursable expenses.

Authority to Commit. If you have chosen a win-win strategy and if you are negotiating with a principal from your client's organization, it is important that you select a member of your team who has the authority to sign the contract. Be careful with regard to the issue of authority, which will be discussed later, because it is a sensitive and important issue to decide in planning your negotiating. If you send an individual to the negotiation session who has the authority to commit, but the client does not, you may be forced to prematurely commit to items that you would otherwise avoid a commitment on. For instance, you might mention a possible multiplier in the negotiation. Anyone on the client's team would certainly pass on such a piece of information to whomever would finalize the agreement. Therefore, protect yourself carefully whenever you have authority and the client does not by refraining from mentioning any specific fixed terms or numbers.

Prior Promises. One of the most overlooked areas in the selection of personnel for the negotiating team is the area of "prior promises." Often during a negotiation you may be reminded of a promise that was made by another sales or marketing person for the design firm that commits the firm to a faster schedule or lesser dollar amount than is presently being negotiated. Without the benefit of having the leadfinder or marketing director in the room, it is impossible for your team to know whether or not the client is bluffing about prior promises.

Thus, it is critical that anyone who could have been in a position to make a prior promise to the client during the sales and marketing of the job be part of the negotiating team. Do not overlook this important item and be certain to cover it as an issue, whether or not you place your marketing director or lead finder on your negotiating team. If they are not chosen to be on the team, it is critical that all promises or statements made to the client prior to the negotiation be documented for use by the negotiating team.

Attorneys. Never place your attorney on a negotiating team. Particularly if you have chosen a win-win strategy, an attorney will not benefit your plan of attack. In fact, because attorneys are hired to defend your best interest, they may work against a win-win strategy by discovering all the unique little twists that are impossible for you to agree to with your client, such as the specific insurance language necessary to assure that your liability coverage remains intact. Should such a situation arise, it is better for you and your client to "agree to agree" with whatever language both of your attorneys work out than to have the attorneys present. For example, should you object to indemnification language in a client contract, rather than calling in attorneys and insurance agents to resolve the language, suggest that your attorney and the client's meet to work out correct language for both. Doing so allows you and your client to avoid being needlessly deadlocked.

Consider how you would feel if you walked into a negotiation in a spirit of true cooperation only to find that your client has an attorney at his or her right hand. Your immediate response would be to take a defensive position and quietly reveal nothing for fear that the attorney will twist and turn your statements in order to hurt you later. Thus, our rule is clear: Never take your attorney to a negotiation session if you have chosen a win-win strategy.

In a win-lose environment this position would change. If you plan to intimidate your client into a loss, you may want your attorney along. But be certain that you understand the implications of bringing your attorney onto the team before indiscriminately adding him or her.

Accountants. Like attorneys, accountants are hired primarily to protect the client whom they serve. Thus, our rule is similar. Do not bring your outside accountant to a negotiation session. Instead, plan to deal with the numbers yourself and caucus for clarification if it is needed. We have often observed smoothly proceeding negotiations run into a road block when an accountant begins to haggle over nickel-and-dime items because he or she must have accuracy in all numbers. Instead of having your accountant present, agree to all general concepts in the negotiation and then pass the final agreement by your accountant for an opinion. Doing so saves you much time and energy and also saves you agony should you place the wrong accountant on your negotiating team.

The Agenda

As part of your planning it is very important that every negotiating session have an agenda. Figure 3-1 shows a typical agenda for a negotiation session.

Note that in Figure 3-1 the agenda is confidential, to be used by your team members only. The client

● Figure 3-1. Typical Agenda for a Negotiation Session

Confidential

*   Goals: To achieve a lump sum fee of $100,000 plus expenses with a 10-month design schedule using subconsultants of our own choice and a definitive schedule of client review meetings with initial commitment to our own suggested project program.

*   Lead Negotiator: John Signore, Project Manager

1. Complete review of scope (lead by John Signore, Project Manager)
    a. Documentation of existing dimensions
    b. Nurse's station redesign
    c. Operating suite renovations
    d. CAT scanner location
    e. Code requirements

*   Take a break to caucus

2. Project financing (led by Dean Whitaker, Principal)
    a. State and federal fund implications
    b. Fund raising drive
    c. Operating versus capital budget implications

3. Project schedule (led by John Signore, Project Manager)
    a. Phasing of doctor and support staff interviews
    b. Hospital review meeting schedule
    c. Construction start date versus financing
    d. Onsite demolition schedule

*   Take time to caucus to discuss pricing

4. Project Team (led by Dean Whitaker, Principal)
    a. Outside consultants
    b. Design team
    c. Client team

5. Pricing (led by John Signore, Project Manager)
    a. Manpower estimates
    b. Reimbursables
    c. Fee
    d. Payment schedule

6. Terms (led by Dean Whitaker, Principal)
    a. Lump sum contract
    b. Reimbursables
    c. Liability
    d. Change orders

7. Written Agreement (led by Tom Smith, Director of Finance)

*   Walk-out Position: Lump sum fee of not less than $75,000 plus expenses with a 7 1/2-month design schedule. Also we must be able to use XYZ mechanical engineers as our HVAC consultant.

should not receive a copy of this agenda, as you would be showing your entire hand going into the negotiation. It is important that each step of the negotiation be planned and that items on the agenda include caucuses, coffeebreaks, interruptions, and other things that will assist you in planning a strategy for your entire session. It is also important that the goals for the negotiation session be placed at the top of the agenda and that your walk-out position be written on the bottom so that every member of your team is vitally aware of the importance of these two items.

The agenda should also identify individuals who are responsible for specific tasks during the negotiation, such as financial commitment, reimbursable terms, or design scope. Note on the sample agenda how names are assigned to specific items. Also, note that the name of the negotiation leader is placed at the top of the agenda. The leader should be in charge of the team and should generate and repeat all questions that are asked of the team prior to delegating the answer to an individual on the team.

A well-planned agenda allows for many caucuses even though a caucus may not be needed. In a win-win environment, take the time needed to analyze and review progress during the negotiation that a caucus is designed to provide. Additional techniques include such minor items as breaking for coffee or breaking to use the bathroom. Keep your agenda simple and attempt to keep it on one page. Never, never reveal it to your client. One specific item to note on our sample agenda is that there is no time limit for any of the negotiating points. Unlike a normal meeting agenda or project agenda, the agenda for a negotiating session has no time limit. If you set a time limit in a negotiating agenda, you will be working against your win-win strategy.

Identifying Specific Sources of Power

During one of your initial meetings to plan the negotiation sessions, identify your team's specific sources of power that will be used during the negotiations. By listing them, you naturally begin to formulate a strategy for the session itself. Ask yourself some of the following questions with regard to the power that you could have on your negotiating team.

❶ Money. Does your firm possess enough money so that money is not important in the negotiation? If it does and if money is not important to the success of the project, it gives your team a source of power.

❷ Time. With time on your side you have incredible power. If the client must have the project within a short duration of time and if you have an unlimited amount of time with which to do the project, you then possess power.

❸ Competition. If there is no competition for the type of work being discussed in this negotiation, it provides you with a unique source of power. Generally there is competition, but through effective marketing you may be able to position your firm so that it is thought of as having no competition. Ask yourself if you have the power of "no competition" in this negotiation.

❹ Experience. Of course, experience is a great teacher. Ask yourself if your team members or your negotiating staff has had prior experience in this type of project. The experience of a prior negotiation with a similar client is invaluable. If there are people in your firm who have negotiated previously with the particular client, they should be part of the planning session to strategize how best to deal with the old client.

❺ Knowledge. A little knowledge goes a long way, but a lot of knowledge gives your team significant power in the negotiation. Does your firm possess a significant amount of specific knowledge of this client type, and is the knowledge required to accomplish the project on schedule?

❻ Negotiating Skill. Does your negotiation team have the power of formal negotiating skill? Has your team taken seminars or gone to school to learn effective negotiating techniques? Has your team read a significant amount of material on how to negotiate? Is the client prepared for the negotiating session, or do you have more power because you have more capability at negotiating as a team?

⑦ Workload. Does your firm have a significant backlog of work? If the answer is yes, you have a source of power with which to negotiate this particular contract. With little or no workload, your power may be stripped away.

⑧ Facts. Have you done a significant amount of research to uncover the right facts about this project and about your negotiating position? Do you have cost data, salary surveys, construction data, or other related material to justify each cost position that you have taken on the project?

⑨ Preparation. Has your team adequately prepared and drilled itself in the technique of handling this specific negotiating session? Has your team had enough prior planning to implement a strategy that will work? Is your agenda set, and have you strategized how each item on the agenda will be handled in the actual session? Have you researched the competition significantly to determine whether or not you have more or less preparation time than they do?

⑩ Commitment. Is your team truly commited to going after the project in a win-win spirit? Does your team have the time to prepare for the negotiation, or are they simply responding whenever a call is made from the client for the negotiation? Have you thought about creative ways to do a negotiating session with this particular client, or has the commitment level been so low that a routine negotiation is at hand?

⑪ Courage. Does your team have the courage to make significant demands upon the client based on the strategy that you have chosen? Likewise, is your team courageous enough to walk out of the negotiation if walkout strategy is necessary? Perhaps the most important part of courage on the negotiating team is the ability to get up and walk out when you have met your low number. Ask yourself if your team has this source of power.

⑫ Appearance. Is your team physically balanced to negotiate with the client? Does it have the right age mix, ethnic mix, and project "gray-hair" mix to be effective? Has your team studied how to dress for negotiations, and are they practicing what they have learned? One of the most subtle but significant aspects of power in a negotiation is the physical appearance of the negotiating team.

⑬ Logistics. Have you planned the room environment for your negotiation, or are you simply responding to whatever the client has planned for you? Are the logistics a source of power because they are on your home turf? Have you done enough research to find out where light switches, heat switches, or telephone jacks are? Logistics can be a source of power for or against you, and your relative position should be understood prior to entering the session itself.

⑭ Stamina. Is your negotiation team in good physical condition? Do they have the stamina to conduct 48 hours of direct negotiations without a break? Are they capable of "hanging in there" when the going gets tough? A lack of stamina can be a significant weakness in a negotiating team if it causes your personnel to commit themselves prematurely. Your firm may lose at the negotiating table because of lack of stamina.

When preparing for your negotiation, make a specific list of responses to the preceding questions and add to it any items of importance with regard to the specific project at hand. Your negotiating power checklist should identify those sources of power that will help you control the negotiation session and lead it toward a win-win solution.

Preparing to Trade

Most design professionals fail to recognize the importance of trading in negotiating. Because of the belief that all clients are honest and because of market pressure to secure a project at all costs, the idea of trading is not a prevalent one at most negotiating sessions. Whenever a client receives something from you, it is always important that you should get something in return. To help you prepare for trading, you should develop three specific lists:

❶ List what you can give up, item by item, with a price attached to each item.

② List what you absolutely cannot give up under any circumstances.

③ List what you want from the client; have a price associated with each item you want.

Note that these three lists are very subjective. This is so because they are important for you to think about what you want in the negotiation before you go in, to know what you cannot give up, and to decide what you can give up. Having these three lists during the preparation for the negotiation helps each member of the team recognize the relative importance of the project to the firm. Figure 3-2 contains examples of the three lists that are mentioned here.

Preparing a trading list is a critical element in the educational process of a negotiating team. By having such a list in front of each of the members of the team, you can be assured that the session will go as planned.

Gathering Data

When planning your negotiating strategy, it is important to either gather data or make an assumption about data on how you will produce the job. We all know that job cost estimates can be produced easily if we are fully aware of specific scope requirements. However,

---

● **Figure 3-2. ABC Hospital Renovations: Three Sample Lists**

Items We Can Give Up

1. Reimbursable travel (since we have another project in the vicinity).
2. Furniture selection (since they have an on-site interiors department).
3. Choice of structural consultant (since minimal structural work is required).
4. Schedule changes to accelerate the project (since we are slow at present).

What We Cannot Give Up

1. Choice of mechanical consultant (since they did the original mechanical design on the project).
2. Choice of project manager (since John Signore is our most experienced hospital project manager).
3. Lump sum contract (since all prior contracts with this client have been lump sum).

What You Want from Client

1. Accurate information from the client with review deadlines met.
2. On-site office space for our project team.
3. Permits and approvals handled by the client.
4. Construction supervision paid for on hourly basis.
5. Reduced liability exposure through an agreement tying our liability to the amount of our fee.
6. A retainer of $10,000 before starting work.

---

in many negotiations, there is no scope yet defined and the client has yet to allocate a schedule or budget to the project. Nonetheless, it is important that any negotiating team prepare a preliminary budget and schedule for the project and collect as much data as possible to justify a position when entering a negotiation. In the absence of a specific scope, use typical data from a prior project as a starting point for discussions. If you have done many similar projects, this data should be readily available. If not, it is still good to attempt an estimate based on your best professional judgment of what it will take to do the job.

Negotiating without appropriate data can only lead to losses. Negotiating with an assumed scope and justifiable cost data to back it up can provide the starting point for a positive session. You can be assured that the client with whom you negotiate has already thought about the scope and the finances necessary to accomplish the project as defined. By the time you sit down in a negotiation, you should have a complete job cost estimate and you should be ready to discuss each item with your client.

Table 3-1 is a typical cost-based estimate form that can be used in the data formulation stage of the planning, while Table 3-2 is a completed cost estimate of a typical government form.

In addition to specific project information, it is important that you collect and have with you enough justifiable data to back up other elements of your negotiation. For instance, have the complete résumé of each project team member at your disposal during the negotiation session together with a complete history of your organization. Financial statements should be with you so that you can refer to them or so that you can use them to justify specific financial positions suggested in the negotiation session. Collecting all data during the preparation for the negotiation is vital. Do not overlook any piece of data simply because you regard it as routine. Remember that the client does not know your organization, and any information to justify a financial or manhour position is vital.

● Table 3-1. Estimating Costs of Architectural Services

ESTIMATING COST OF ARCHITECTURAL SERVICES

FIRM:

CLIENT:

PROJECT:

	AIA Doc. B141			PRINCIPAL Time Rate		EMPLOYEE Time Rate		CONSULTANT Time Rate	
FEASIBILITY	1.3.1	Additional	Project Programming						
	1.3.2		Economic Feasibility Analysis & Reports						
	1.3.2		Promotional, Fund Raising or Other Special Studies						
	1.3.3		Master Planning						
	1.3.3		Site Evaluation and Selection						
	1.3.3		Environmental Impact Studies						
			Administrative Services/Conferences						
			SUB TOTALS:						
SCHEMATIC	1.1.1	Basic	Program Review						
	1.1.2		Architectural Schematic Design Studies						
	1.1.2		Engineering Systems Analysis						
	1.1.3		Statement of Probable Construction Cost						
			Administrative Services/Conferences						
	1.3.4	Add.	Design Services Relative to Future Facilities						
	1.3.5		Existing Building Surveys						
			SUB TOTALS:						
DESIGN DEVELOPMENT	1.1.4	Basic	Architectural Design Development						
	1.1.4		Structural Design Development						
	1.1.4		Mechanical Design Development						
	1.1.4		Electrical Design Development						
	1.1.5		Statement of Probable Construction Cost						
			Administrative Services/Coordination						
	1.3.5	Add.	Preparation of Measured Drawings						
			SUB TOTALS:						
CONSTRUCTION DOCUMENTS	1.1.6	Basic	Architectural Working Drawings						
	1.1.6		Structural Working Drawings						
	1.1.6		Civil Working Drawings						
	1.1.6		Mechanical Working Drawings						
	1.1.6		Electrical Working Drawings						
	1.1.6		Specifications and General Conditions						
	1.1.7		Final Statement of Probable Construction Cost						
	1.1.8		Governmental/Regulatory Agency Approvals						
			Administrative Services/ Coordination						
	1.3.6	Addn 1.	Documents for Alternate Bids or other Special Bid Documents						
	1.3.7		Detailed Estimates of Construction Costs						
	1.3.7		Detailed Quantity Surveys of Inventories						
	1.3.8		Interior Design						
	1.3.8		Furniture Selection or Special Fixture Design						
	1.3.9		Planning Tenant or Rental Space						
	1.3.10		Drawing Revisions Inconsistent with Prior Approvals						
			SUB TOTALS:						

53

	AIA Doc. B141			PRINCIPAL Time Rate		EMPLOYEE Time Rate		CONSULTANT Time Rate	
BID & NEGOTIATIONS	1.1.9	Basic	Bidding/Negotiation						
	1.1.9		Addenda and Drawing Revisions						
	1.1.9		Construction Agreement						
		Add	Administrative Services/Coordination						
	1.3.10		Drawing Revision Inconsistent with Prior Approvals						
			SUB TOTALS:						
CONSTRUCTION	1.1.11	Basic	Construction Contract Administration/Conferences						
	1.1.14		Construction Observations						
	1.1.15		Job Cost Accounting/Certification						
	1.1.16		Clarifications						
	1.1.17		Testing and Inspection Coordinating						
	1.1.18		Shop Drawing and Submittal Review						
	1.1.19		Quotation Request/Review/Change Orders						
	1.1.20		Substantial Completions						
	1.1.20		Final Acceptance						
	1.2.1	Addn'l	Administrative Services/Conferences						
	1.3.11		Full Time Project Representation						
	1.3.12		Preparing Supporting Data etc. on Change Orders						
	1.3.13		Investigations/Evaluations re: Owner Work						
	1.1.14		Replacement Work re: Fire or Other Causes						
			Services Required Due to Contractor Work Defects or Default						
			SUB TOTALS:						
POST CONSTRUCTION	1.3.15	Addn'l	As Built Drawings						
	1.3.16		Maintenance and Operational Programming						
	1.3.17		Services After Issuance of Final Certificate for Payment						
OTHER SERVICES	1.3.18	Addn'l	Expert Witness						
	1.3.19		Special Consultants						
	1.3.20		Services Not Customarily in Agreement						
	1.3.20		Other						
			SUB TOTALS:						
REIMBURSABLE EXPENSE	5.1.1		Travelling Transportation & Living Expenses						
			Long Distance Calls						
			Permit Fees						
	5.1.2		Reproduction of Drawings & Specifications, Postage & Handling						
	5.1.3		Overtime Work						
	5.1.3		Renderings and Models						
	5.1.4		Computer Time for Basic Services						
	5.1.5		Computer Time for Additional Services						
			SUB TOTALS:						
OWNER'S RESPONSIBILITY EXPENSE	2.3		Certified Land Survey						
	2.4		Soil Borings, Percolation Tests, Etc.						
	2.5		Quality Control & Testing						
	2.6		Project: Legal, Accounting, Insurance Services						
			SUB TOTALS:						
			TOTALS:						

● Table 3-1. Continued

COMPREHENSIVE ARCHITECTURAL SERVICES

Compensation for architectural services varies widely with the complexity of the project and the scope of services performed by the Architect. Usual methods of compensation include the following:

> Multiple of Direct Personnel Expense
> Professional Fee plus Expense
> Percentage of Construction Cost
> Fixed Sum

Each of these methods has advantages for specific types of projects as discussed more fully in AIA Document B551: Statement of the Architect's Services.

Although compensation may be quoted in different ways, it is necessarily based on the time and costs required to perform a given service; therefore, the scope of architectrual services will be in direct relation to the compensation provided.

This document is intended to be used in conjunction with AIA Document B551: Statement of the Architect's Services and AIA Document B141: Owner-Architect Agreement, which sets forth the architect's services to the client.

Because of the broad range of services often required to establish, design and complete the client's project, it is recommended that a detailed review of the services by phase be made before the execution of the client-architect agreement, along with an estimate of time required for the project. The agreement should reflect the possible extension of services and should accommodate services found to be needed after the project has been started.

The list of Comprehensive Architectural Services, included herein and which is not all-inclusive, is intended to assist the client in understanding the full scope of effort and time which may be required of the architect and his consultants. It serves to:

1) Organize in a coherent manner the tasks and responsibilities for all major elements of activity for a given project:

2) Provide a detailed summary of the cost estimate for major elements of the project and may be used both for negotiation as well as project monitoring; and

3) Provide a detailed record for in-house project cost control available for review with the client.

This list of Comprehensive Architectural Services is developed directly from the Owner-Architect Agreement, AIA Document B141, and each item is identified as either a basic or additional service and referenced in the document by paragraph number.

● Table 3-2. Example of a Form Used to Summarize Costs Associates with Design Projects

U. S. ARMY
HUNTSVILLE DIVISION, CORPS OF ENGINEERS

ARCHITECT-ENGINEER COST ESTIMATE	ARCHITECT-ENGINEER FIRM NAME AND ADDRESS		DESIGN STAGE		COST OR PRICING DATA REFERENCE
	ABC Consultants, Inc. 1000 Main Street Anytown, USA		MODIFIED CONCEPT	(OPTION) FINAL	
RFP/CONTR. NUMBER DACA87- 81 - R - 0000			**LOCATION:** Fort Kennedy		
PREPARED BY: David Smith	**PROJ. TITLE:** Industrial Waste Treatment Facility		**PROJ. NO:** 5062.61		
APPROVED BY: A. W. Jones	**DATE:** 11/8/82	**TASK NAME/BUILDING/OTHER:** Intermediate Design		**TASK NO:**	

ITEM "A"-TASK EFFORT BREAKDOWN   TASK RECAP: 4,024   MH = $ 133,674

SPECIALITIES	JOB TITLES	MAN-HOURS	RATES $	AMOUNTS $	TOTALS $	
PROJECT MANAGEMENT	Supervisor	214	20.50	4,387		
	Typist/Clerical	80	5.89	471	4,858	
CIVIL	Supervisor	10	20.50	205		
	Journeyman	30	13.89	417		
	Draftsman	90	8.90	801		
NO. OF DWGS.(3)	Typist	20	5.89	118	1,541	
ARCHITECTURAL	Supervisor	14	20.50	287		
	Journeyman	30	13.89	417		
	Designer	48	10.95	526		
NO. OF DWGS.(4)	Typist	12	5.89	71	1,301	
STRUCTURAL	Supervisor	34	20.50	697		
	Journeyman	100	13.89	1,389		
	Draftsman	280	8.90	2,492		
NO. OF DWGS.(7)	Typist	24	5.89	141	4,719	
MECHANICAL	Supervisor	232	20.50	4,756		
	Journeyman	928	13.89	12,890		
	Designer	996	10.95	10,906		
NO. OF DWGS.(36)	Typist	32	5.89	188	28,740	
HV/AC	Supervisor	6	20.50	123		
	Journeyman	20	13.89	278		
	Draftsman	30	8.90	267		
NO. OF DWGS.(2.)	Typist	4	5.89	24	692	
ENVIRONMENTAL	Supervisor	25	20.50	513		
	Journeyman	98	13.89	1,361		
	Draftsman	100	8.90	890		
NO. OF DWGS.(13)	Typist	20	5.89	118	2,882	
ELECTRICAL	Supervisor	63	20.50	1,292		
	Journeyman	85	13.89	1,181		
	Designer	110	10.95	1,205		
NO. OF DWGS.(11)	Typist	16	5.89	256	3,934	
SPECIFICATIONS	Supervisor	28	20.50	574		
	Journeyman	79	13.89	1,097		
	Typist	44	5.89	259	1,930	
ESTIMATES	Supervisor	20	20.50	410		
	Journeyman	102	13.89	1,417	1,827	
OTHER						
TOTAL DRAWINGS 71	**TOTAL MAN-HOURS** 4,024			**TOTAL DIRECT SALARIES**	52,424	

ITEM "B" OVERHEAD POOLS

	TITLES	RATES %	BASES $			
1	Total Allowable Overhead	148.3	52,424		77,745	
2						
3						

ITEM "C" OTHER COST (CONSULTANTS ,TELEPHONE, REPRODUCTION, POSTAGE, ATTACH ESTIMATES AS REQUIRED	1,252
ITEM "D" TRAVEL COST (ATTACH ESTIMATE SHEETS)	2,253
ITEM "E" MATERIAL AND SUPPIES (ATTACH ESTIMATES AS REQUIRED)	

HND FORM 371   14 AUG 1975

Researching the Other Side. Now that you have a client and now that you are about to enter the negotiating phase of the project, it is important for you to gather all available information on your client and your client's finances. Much of this information may have already been collected by your marketing staff. However, be careful not to take all data provided by marketing at face value, since much of it may have been manipulated for sales purposes to encourage a favorable interpretation and to strengthen chances for selection. One of the best sources of information about your client or opposition in a negotiation is to check with prior clients or bank references. Bank references can give you an objective view of the client, including any limitations that may have been placed on the client by the bank. In addition, attorneys or accountants in the community can assist by providing you subjective information about the client.

Keep track of past clients. It is also good to discuss any new client with other design professionals. Many unscrupulous clients "run through" design firms at a rapid pace, leaving a trail of disasters behind them. Therefore, you can communicate your success at being selected to as many people as possible and at the same time discuss how to negotiate with this client with as many friendly competitors as you can find.

Another source of information on clients is your consulting staff. Interior designers and structural engineers provide perhaps the best source of information on clients available in the marketplace, since both disciplines work extensively for other design professionals. Check with other local professionals during your planning stage to determine whether or not your new client is worth the effort.

Cost Data

One of the most vital elements in preparing for any negotiation is the collection of cost data to justify your financial position. More important than justifying your own project position is the importance of objective outside data to justify salary rates and other issues. For the purposes of cost data, your firm should be up to date with the latest salary survey information administered by several nationally renowned companies. Table 3-3 shows a number of salary surveys available together with the name and address of the publisher.

Surveys are also conducted by many state and local chapters of the American Institute of Architects (AIA), American Consulting Engineers Council (ACEC), and the National Society of Professional Engineers (NSPE). For instance, the Boston Society of Architects conducts an annual salary survey of its 453 members.

In addition to cost data for salaries alone, it may be important to justify your multiplier or another aspect of your overhead for the client. Doing so may require the use of outside information to assist you in supporting a claim for a high multiplier or high overhead figure. There are many national surveys available on financial statistics for design firms and we recommend that you obtain at least one recent copy of a nationwide survey. Using surveys to justify your position in a negotiating session puts you in a strong position.

● **Table 3-3. Salary Surveys of Design Professionals**

Survey	Source
Marketing Salary Survey (annual)	Society of Marketing Professional Services (SMPS) 1437 Powhatan Street Alexandria, VA 22314
Survey of Salaries in Landscape Architecture Firms	American Society of Landscape Architects (ASLA) 1733 Connecticut Avenue, N.W. Washington, DC 20009
Executive Management Salary Survey (annual)	PSMJ Surveys Professional Services Management Journal 126 Harvard Street Brookline, MA 02146
Various engineering salary surveys	D. Dietrich Associates, Inc. P.O. Box 511 Phoenixville, PA 19460

Unless the other side has done enough research to understand totally the salary surveys, compensation surveys, or financial management surveys that you propose during your negotiating session, it will be impossible for them to overcome your position.

The collection and use of cost data is one of the most important items in planning for a negotiation. Your firm should maintain a current library of all surveys done in the area of project costing and financial costing to be certain that this information is at your fingertips in planning for a rapid negotiating session. Never enter into a negotiation without a significant amount of third-party supporting data to justify your cost figures. If this is not done, your client may suspect that you are arbitrarily choosing your numbers without regard to their needs.

Preparation Techniques

As part of your planning, schedule a series of negotiation preparation meetings or dry runs. Each negotiation preparation meeting should feature a mock negotiation to depict the real circumstances of the project that you are negotiating. Many firms today are even videotaping the negotiating and marketing presentations done by their staff to improve the quality of individual behavior traits needed in a negotiation. Consider the logistics of the situation and the people involved in the negotiation to determine whether or not additional mock negotiations are needed.

A mock negotiation gives you the chance to judge how effective your negotiators are while giving an opportunity for new, younger employees to join the ranks of those who are already negotiating. In addition, it is important that every member of the negotiation team prepare for negotiating by reading this book. The Selected Bibliography lists many recent articles that are worthy of study.

Flight/Hotel Rooms

Some of the most overlooked elements in planning for a negotiation are the nitty-gritty details of getting there and getting back. How often have we heard the story of a design team missing a negotiating session simply because they missed their flight. It is imperative, therefore, that in your planning you anticipate how you are going to get to the negotiation, where you will stay, how you will eat, and what you will bring with you for the effectiveness of the program.

Do not leave this aspect of planning until the last minute, as you could miss your negotiation should an airline schedule be sold out. Instead, as part of your initial planning session, assign the task of getting flights and hotel accommodations to a secretary who will immediately fulfill the requirements. To say that you have missed your plane is no excuse to a client, and it may well place you in a losing position.

Audiovisual Preparation

Understand what you will require for audiovisual and logistical support during your negotiating session. For instance, will you require any audiovisual equipment to show slides or overhead projections to illustrate a point in your negotiation? As part of your planning, make a complete list of requirements for audiovisual and logistical assistance during your negotiating session. Some of the items to consider bringing include:

1. Flip chart and easel
2. Magic markers
3. Masking tape
4. Slide or overhead projectors
5. Spare bulbs
6. Extension cords
7. Pointers
8. Notepads and pencils
9. Microphones
10. Tape or video recorders and players
11. Pens, pencils, erasers
12. Index cards
13. Surveys

Determining Your Client's Power

Part of the planning for a successful negotiation includes enough research about your client to identify the client's weaknesses and strengths. The client's power can be determined by checking both financial and community references. For instance, does the client really have financing on the project? Are they talking with other design professionals, or are you the only design firm being interviewed? What happens if the client doesn't sign with you? In the case of government negotiators, this may mean that they must fill out reams of reports to justify going to another design firm after having failed at the negotiation session with you. Do they need you and only you? Do they have enough charisma and personal power in the negotiation session itself?

One of the most critical issues to discuss during planning for the negotiation is your client's biases against you. Collect as much data as possible from your marketing people about your client's biases during the selection process. Did your client object to the distance that your office is from their office? Was a bad reference uncovered during the marketing of the job? Has your own inexperience at doing this type of work been held against you during the presentation for the job? Is your price too high? Do you have too much or too little quality demonstrated in your proposal?

List for each client the specific requirements that you believe they expect to achieve in the negotiation session. Doing so allows you to determine whether the client wants a "gold-plated Mercedes" project or a "beat-up Chevrolet" project. Often we observe that design firms enter a negotiation without determining the client's power, strengths, weaknesses, or biases against the firm. In addition, many design professionals simply do not perceive or list any of the client's real requirements prior to beginning the negotiation.

Your Written Plan

Just like a marketing presentation, the preparation for a negotiation session should include a written plan. The plan should have a schedule assigned to it and specific assignments for each member of the team. A planning schedule during the negotiation preparation assures that all elements of the preparation are accomplished. Table 3-4 shows a sample negotiating schedule that a typical interior design firm used to achieve a successful negotiation with a condominium developer.

● Table 3-4. Sample Negotiating Schedule

PROJECT: Sunshine Condominium Development
CLIENT: ACE Development Corporation
LEAD NEGOTIATOR: Tom Phillips

Date	Task	Team Personnel Involved
January 18	Identify location of negotiation session.	RCV
January 22	Develop specifics of what scope of project should be.	TLP
January 24	Initial negotiating team meeting takes place.	TLP
January 24	Assign tasks prior to negotiation session.	TLP
January 25	Airline/hotel reservations made.	SJL
January 25	Audiovisual checklist prepared.	DAR
January 26	Logistical research report done.	SJL
January 26	Client finance research done.	TLP
January 26	Initial scope/schedule prepared. Outline and handouts planned.	TLP/RCV
January 28	Negotiating team meets to set agenda for the negotiation.	TLP
January 30	First mock negotiation takes place.	TLP and team
February 1	Presentation is adjusted.	All
February 2	Second mock negotiation takes place.	TLP and team
February 4	Actual negotiation begins.	All

Note that the planning schedule includes practice sessions, development of handouts, a series of decision points and indicates the name of the negotiation leader. Each element is important to plan, and having the plan allows all members of the team to focus their energies on a more effective negotiation session, no matter what strategy you choose.

How to Run Mock Negotiations

As part of your preparation for a negotiation session, there should be a minimum of two practice sessions. Practice sessions allow the entire negotiating team to role play their agenda and to improve their specific negotiating techniques prior to entering the actual negotiation. In addition, having practice sessions helps the firm identify potential new negotiators from the ranks of those within the firm. To do so, make the negotiating practice session as real as possible by telling each team that they may change a specific rule in the negotiation without telling the other team what rule they have changed. For example, tell the mock client to cut the scope of work in half without informing your team and then watch how they respond. Or tell the mock client to insist on a different type of contract than you want, and see if your negotiators are effective at convincing the client to do it your way. Also, for the most effective practice session, tell each team to initiate the session with a strategy of win-lose in mind. The most difficult strategy to overcome and in which to achieve a win-win solution is a win-lose strategy. By structuring your practice session to begin with win-lose strategies, the worst strategies of both teams can be identified and the strengths of those negotiators on your team to persist in finding a win-win solution can be observed. Conduct practice sessions in as real a setting as possible, preferably outside your office, so that full concentration can be on the negotiation itself. Consider videotaping practice sessions if you feel that will assist those in the negotiation session to analyze their performance better.

Be Prepared

Not enough can be said about the importance of preparing for the actual negotiation. Of course, you must weigh the amount and cost of planning against the anticipated fee that you will achieve by negotiating the project at hand. When doing so, however, be prepared to invest enough time to educate your staff, to prepare for specific objections of the client, and to achieve the strategy that you set out to achieve at the beginning of your negotiation session.

Planning is one of the most important activities that a good negotiator must engage in. Having an agenda, preparing for who should go, and listing all the logistical requirements, together with collecting data on the client, is vitally important to the success of the entire negotiating process. And remember, the lack of a plan may lead to disaster.

4 Shaping the Negotiation

- Are the room and table shape really important?

- How can you control heat, noise, and light?

- How should you seat yourselves to maximize your strategy choice?

- Who should start a negotiating session?

- Are interruptions effective as a negotiating technique?

- Are there ways to overcome negative logistics?

- What if you cannot get data on where you will negotiate?

One of the most important but least understood aspects of a negotiation is the impact of logistical considerations. Many people believe that the shape of the table, the heat in the room, the lighting conditions, and other physical aspects of the negotiation are unimportant. However, it has been shown through various studies that logistics play a bigger role than most people think. One of the most famous confirmations of this fact is that it took six months to decide on the shape of the table for the Paris Peace talks, which dealt with the Vietnam War. Thus, logistics are important, and in this chapter we will provide several examples of how logistics can work positively for you in an architecture/engineering firm negotiation.

Room Size and Location

Prior to planning and negotiation, it is important that the room in which the negotiation will be held be completely analyzed. Although this may seem inappropriate, consider that the shape of the room and the size of the room may have an impact either positively or negatively on the feelings that your own negotiating staff will have. To quickly understand the importance of room size and shape, recall in your mind the last time you visited a high school classroom. Think about the furnishings that were in that schoolroom, including the blackboard, the school chairs, wastebaskets, the teacher's desk, and other materials that are typically familiar in a high school classroom. Now ask yourself how that room would be lit. Would there be flourescent lighting or incandescent lighting? Would there be windows on one side of the room? How would you negotiate in such a room?

Having thought about a high school classroom, picture in your mind the last time you were in a judge's chambers. Think about the typical furnishings there. Is there a bench? Are there pews? Are there elaborate wood tables? Are the doors in the center of the room at the rear? Is there a flag? Are there padded chairs in various sections of the room? Is there a noticeable absence of windows?

● Checklist 4-1. Logistics of the Negotiating Room

○ Exact dimension of the room (length, width, height)._____

○ Surface finishes of the room (floor, walls, ceilings)._____

○ Number and placement of windows._____

○ East/west orientation (for sun conditions)._____

○ Lighting conditions and type of lights._____

○ Furnishings (permanent and/or nonpermanent)._____

○ Location of telephones and types of telephones._____

○ Location and type of light switches._____

○ Location of heat controls and how they operate._____

○ Door locking and key locations._____

○ Type and use of adjoining rooms._____

○ Proximity to copiers, men's and ladies' rooms, secretarial help.

○ Availability of audiovisual materials._____

○ Other activities occurring at the same time of day your meeting will occur._____

There is no doubt that the nature of a negotiation in a high school classroom would be totally different from a negotiation in a judge's chambers. Such a comparison indicates the relative importance of researching the room that you will use for the negotiation. Use Checklist 4-1 to research the existing logistical nature of the negotiating room.

Checklist 4-1 should be used when researching a location for negotiation. Establish a questionnaire and send an individual who will be part of the negotiation to research the logistical aspects of the meeting room. Using Checklist 4-1, let's consider the importance of each item that you will research and the potential for circumstances that could occur if that item is not researched.

Table Shape   Where you sit at the negotiating table can determine to a great extent which strategic position you must acquire in the negotiation. There are four different table shapes that are most commonly used:

1. Square
2. Rectangular
3. Circular
4. Oval

To best analyze where to sit at any of the four tables or which of the four table shapes to use in a negotiation, let us examine each table shape and the various positions of sitting at each table with respect to the four strategic choices that are outlined in Chapter 2. The most complicated arrangements are involved in the win-win strategy.

Win-Win Strategy: Square Table. Under a win-win strategy, the positioning of your seat at a square table is critical. You should always sit at the right hand of the power of the party with whom you are negotiating. This means that if there are two of you in the negotiation, you should sit right next to the individual with whom you are negotiating. Remember that one of the colloquialisms in our language is to sit "at the right hand of the boss." This colloquialism has significant meaning since several studies have shown that those sitting at the right hand of the boss end up taking over for the boss sooner or later. In a negotiation, the win-win strategy is best achieved by *not* sitting directly opposite someone. This creates an atmosphere of antagonism instead of cooperation. Therefore, the optimum position is at the right hand of the power.

Of course, if there are more than two people in the negotiation, it is important to find out who has the power before choosing your seat. "Power" can be defined as the charismatic quality of the individual within the organization who wields the most power, not necessarily the individual who has the highest ranking title. Do not be afraid to move seats and to change positions if the position you are placed in by your client would be disadvantageous for a win-win strategy. It is better to jokingly suggest that you want to be close to the boss, than to allow yourself to be positioned in an opposing seat, which may lead to a win-lose result.

Win-Win Strategy: Rectangular Table. The rules that apply to a square table apply to a rectangular table as well. It is always important to sit at the right hand of the power if you have chosen a win-win strategy. A further complexity introduced by a rectangular table is that when you are positioned at an opposing end, the length of the table enhances the possibility for a win-lose situation.

Figure 4-1 illustrates a situation that is rather typical with rectangular tables. Whenever there are two to six people in the negotiation, it is often common to position one team along one side of the rectangular table and another team on the opposite side. Under a win-win strategy, we recommend that you do not allow this to occur. It is better to intermingle your people among your client's than to have your entire team sitting on one side of the table and their team on the other. Of course, the complexity created by intermingling people is that your notes may be seen by the opposing negotiating team and their notes may be seen by yours. However, under a win-win strategy the seating decision may be more important than confidentiality in achieving the desired outcome.

Win-Win Strategy: Circular Table. The optimum table shape for a win-win negotiation is a circular table. The circular table presents no corners on which the opposing party can place you. Likewise, sitting around a circular table allows for the most openness of communication in a negotiation. Psychologically we are more open to discuss things with an individual at a round table than at any other shaped table. Therefore, if you are in a position to choose the table shape for a win-win strategy negotiation, always choose a circular table. The only time that a circular table can be negative in a win-win situation is when the table is so large and the number of negotiators are so small that people are placed opposite each other at the table. If this occurs, sit beside the negotiating team with whom you are working instead of across the table.

Win-Win Strategy: Oval Table. The characteristics of an oval table are similar to those of a rectangular table in a win-win strategy session. Be certain not to position yourself opposite individuals with whom you are negotiating. Instead intermingle your staff with those of the client's staff.

Overall, under a win-win strategy, the best approach is to counteract being opposite the client. By this we mean that you should get as close to your client as possible, sitting on the right-hand side of the power. No matter what table shape you use, sitting close to your client inspires closer communication.

Win-Lose and Lose-Win Strategies. For both win-lose and lose-win strategies, the choice of position at the table is clear. Do exactly the opposite of what you would do for a win-win strategy. By this we mean that you should sit opposite your client. Seat yourself on the other end of the table at a rectangular table.

Seat yourself across the circle at a circular table or at the other end of an oval table. By sitting in an opposing position, you are in a sense opposing the strategy of your client's negotiating team. This generally implies that one of the parties will win and the other will lose. Of course, since negotiating is not an exact science, anything can happen. However, the initial encounter at the table can go a long way toward determining the final outcome.

Under a win-lose strategy, position yourself always opposite your client, and try to place barriers on the table such as wine bottles, napkin racks, or books that further the sense of distance between you and the client. Figure 4-2 shows a situation in which a win-lose sitting pattern is structured for the negotiation.

If you find yourself seated opposite your client, but you have chosen a win-win strategy, move to another seat (as shown in Figure 4-3). It is your responsibility to control the logistics when you walk into the room. Do anything possible to change the opposing position. This may mean that you can introduce audiovisual equipment such as a chalkboard or slides that require the client to get up to use them. It can also mean that you change the room entirely, unless the furniture is fixed to the floor. Do not allow yourself to be placed in a win-lose situation if you want a win-win strategy just because the furniture prescribes that mode.

Lose-Lose Strategy. Under a lose-lose situation, the issue of equality is important. Under all circumstances treat a lose-lose situation in a way similar to that of a win-win one from the point of view of table shape. If you find during a negotiation that it is becoming a lose-lose situation when you have chosen a win-lose strategy, notice whether or not you have moved your position at the table to encourage that lose-lose atmosphere.

Unusual Circumstances. It would be nice if there were only four table shapes to deal with. However, there are many unusual circumstances that require

● Figure 4-2. Round Table Win-Lose Seating Pattern

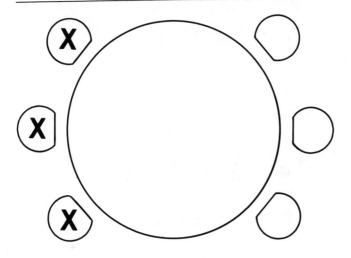

● Figure 4-3. Round Table Win-Win Seating Pattern

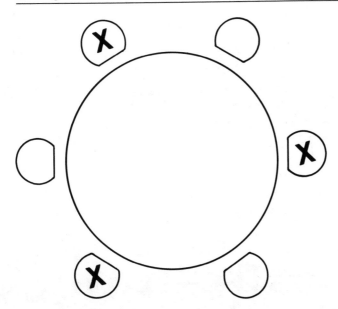

Figure 4-4. Plan View of an Impossible Logistical Situation

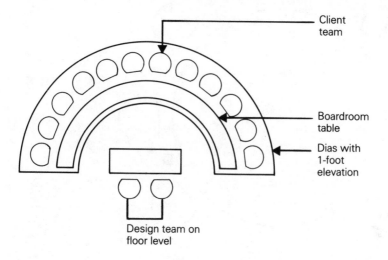

Client team

Boardroom table

Dias with 1-foot elevation

Design team on floor level

Figure 4-5. Changing a Win-Lose Fixed Horseshoe into a Win-Win Situation Using Audiovisual Accessories

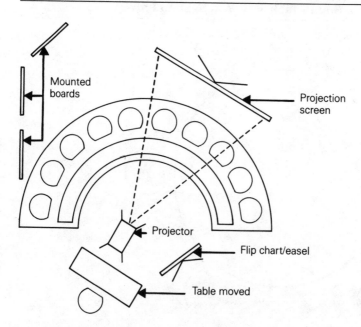

Mounted boards

Projection screen

Projector

Flip chart/easel

Table moved

that you develop a strategy that is consistent with your overall negotiation stance. For instance, have you ever entered a negotiating session in which the shape of the table is a horseshoe elevated above the floor level around which are seated 14 community leaders, while your team is positioned behind a small square table in the middle of the horseshoe? Figure 4-4 depicts this situation. What can you do to overcome the win-lose nature of such a situation?

There are several alternatives for you to consider. First, you must recognize that such a circumstance sets up an absolute win-lose situation. It is so because you have been placed in opposing positions. The client is raised above your level. In addition to being placed at the focal point of a U-shaped table, you are outnumbered. Thus, the first solution is to attempt to change the logistics and remove yourself from the focal point. If the tables are all cemented to the floor, determine an alternate strategy. For instance, bring hanging boards to be placed around the outside (at the back) of the U-shaped table on the wall. Doing so requires that the client turn around to view the items you explain. It also allows you to stand and walk around behind the client, taking yourself out of the focal point of the horseshoe.

Carry with you a flip chart and easel that can be positioned anywhere in the room. Then ask a member of the client team to walk to the easel and demonstrate to you a piping layout, an architectural floor plan, or another aspect of the project. Doing so requires that the client get out of a seat and walk within the U-shaped area, thus placing him or her closer to you and helping to create a win-win logistical situation. Another alternative would be to use a slide projector that requires a rear projection screen or an off-centered projection screen. Figure 4-5 shows the positioning of audiovisual equipment to take you out of a focal position in a U-shaped table, allowing you to achieve a win-win strategy instead of a win-lose one.

Whatever the table shape, it is important to consider your strategy and how it is affected by table shape. Remember that the "opposition" position produces a win-lose strategy at the outset and that the "cooperation and proximity" position produces a win-win or a lose-lose attitude initially.

The crucial element to remember, however, is not to allow yourself to be controlled by the shape of the table without realizing the impact of its shape on your overall negotiation plan.

Lighting

Lighting is one of the most misunderstood aspects in negotiations. How often have you entered a negotiation without considering the impact of the lighting type on your team? In your research and planning for the negotiation, determine what type of lighting is used in the room. The psychological impact of fluorescent lights is significantly different than the impact of 60-watt incandescent bulbs. Warmth and comfort are inspired with incandescent lighting, whereas coolness and discomfort are inspired by fluorescent lighting. Again, for the strategy you choose, consider the impact of lighting. Based on our discussion so far, it should be apparent that a warm and comfortable feeling should be created whenever you want to encourage cooperation in a win-win or lose-lose situation.

Whenever you want opposition to occur in the negotiation, negotiate in a room lighted by fluorescent lamps or in a room that has a significant amount of outdoor light shining directly into it. Brightness produces glare, and glare reduces comfort. In addition, fluorescent light makes an individual feel uncomfortable. Have you ever walked into a department store lit by fluorescent bulbs only to feel self-conscious about the color of your skin or your overall appearance? Sunlight can also be extremely difficult to work with in a negotiation. We have observed circumstances in which a western setting sun shined directly into the eyes of the opposition, creating an uncomfortable, unpleasant atmosphere and thus a win-lose situation. Whenever you examine a room, determine exactly where the sunlight will enter and position yourself appropriately depending on your strategy.

The importance of lighting should never be minimized. For a win-win or lose-lose position, create a comfortable, homogeneous atmosphere with lighting that is appropriate to the circumstances. For a win-lose or lose-win circumstance, create a cold, harsh lighting atmosphere that adds to discomfort. In all cases, know exactly how to control the atmosphere to your best advantage. Determine where light switches are located, where shade pulls are located, or how curtains can be drawn. If you are positioned by a client into a win-lose circumstance, recognize that it exists and take immediate steps to change it prior to beginning the negotiation. Such steps may even include requesting that the room be changed entirely because of the lighting.

Heating

Room temperature is one of the most vital ingredients in a successful negotiation. If your strategy is win-win, the heating level in the negotiating room should be kept at a temperature between 68° and 74° Fahrenheit (F). Any temperature above 74°F makes both parties to the negotiation uncomfortable. If your strategy is win-lose, place the temperature between 60° and 68°. Doing so allows you to prepare in advance for the cool temperature while the opposing party is uncomfortable.

Of course, planning for a specific temperature range requires understanding of exactly how heat is controlled in the meeting room to be used for the negotiation. Thus, as part of your preplanning, find out where all heat controls are located and how to use them. Be especially cognizant of the impact of sunlight and other factors on heating loads within the room. Also, find out where water fountains are located, and ask if water will be available during the negotiation.

Check the humidity level of the room very carefully. The humidity range should be between 50 and 60 percent to provide the optimum level of comfort. Again, if your strategy is win-win, you are seeking optimum comfort. If your strategy is win-lose, you will want to adjust the humidity level downward or upward to create the level of discomfort you desire. Although these recommendations may seem contrived and unethical, remember that the issue of comfort is important to a win-win situation. A win-win negotiation requires a longer time in a meeting room, and thus the temperature is critical for a successful session.

Noise

Probably the most overlooked aspect of planning for a successful negotiation is the noise level within the meeting space. As part of your research, determine what noise level exists within the space naturally. Are there cars passing outside a window? Is there typing noise coming from outside the meeting room? Do telephones ring occasionally within the room?

If extraneous noise permeates the room on a regular basis and if you can control the decibel level within the room, you may wish to "pipe in" background music or subliminal noise to reduce the impact of the natural noise level within the room. We all know that noise can interrupt the most successful meetings, and in a negotiation session a loud clap of thunder or an automobile accident outside of the room may come at the most inappropriate time for a win-win solution. Take steps in your planning to provide enough background noise or to screen out unwanted external noise so that it does not interrupt the most important part of a deal.

If you choose a win-lose strategy, you may want to do the opposite of these recommendations. You may wish to introduce extraneous noise at a planned time to create a distraction. Such noises could include the slamming of doors outside the room or a telephone ringing within the room. All these distractions should be planned to be as natural as possible so that your opposing party does not suspect you of contriving to interrupt the meeting. Of course, it is rather difficult to construct a clap of thunder or an automobile accident, but with some creativity you can easily duplicate natural noises within your environment that will disrupt the client without disturbing you, since you will know that they are coming.

Planned Interruptions

One of the most disturbing occurrences in a negotiation is an unwanted interruption. In a negotiation with a hospital several years ago, I was rudely introduced to the impact of a planned interruption. After having rescheduled our negotiating session several times, the chairman of the hospital board, who was chief executive of a manufacturing company, was scheduled to meet with me at 2 P.M. on a Wednesday afternoon. Arriving promptly at 1:30 so that I would be sure to be on time for the negotiation session, I was left to wait in an outer office until 3 P.M. As soon as we sat down in his office to negotiate the multiplier on direct labor for our hospital renovation contract, there was a knock on the door. A supervisor from the manufacturing assembly line asked if the chairman could come to the line for a brief question. Forty-five minutes later, at approximately 4 P.M., the client returned. All this time I was forced to sit in his office with all my materials and wait.

After we restarted our negotiations and proceeded for approximately 10 minutes, the phone rang. Upon answering the call, the client asked if I would leave the room and wait in the outer lobby, since the telephone call was an urgent and confidential call from Europe that he had awaited for three days. Approximately one hour later I was asked to return to the negotiating table. By this time it was 5 P.M. and the manufacturing facility was closing. Because it was winter, it was also getting dark outside. After a short amount of time the client gave me an ultimatum for the multiplier we were seeking. Since we had already started work and since this was the fourth scheduled meeting with this particular individual, I was forced to accept the ultimatum. Only after several months did I ask this particular individual if the interruptions that occurred during our negotiation were planned. He simply smiled and put his arm around my shoulder, indicating that he had taught me a valuable lesson in negotiating.

Planned interruptions can be one of the most powerful tools in a negotiation session. Unfortunately, whenever you schedule a planned interruption, it must appear as natural as possible to succeed. If a planned interruption appears contrived or whimsical, it will tip off the other party that you are attempting to manipulate the negotiation session. Therefore, brainstorm about the natural daily interruptions of your office procedures. If the negotiation is to occur within your office, are there natural interruptions that could be used to create an appropriate disturbance in the negotiation? If you travel to another site, plan interruptions that require you to use the telephone, the bathroom, or any other facility such as a copy machine so that your negotiation can have breaks within it for you to caucus and discuss new ideas.

Remember that a caucus is a planned interruption within the negotiation that your negotiating team can request. It is perfectly fine for you to ask for a caucus so that you can discuss a new idea or a term to be presented to the opposing party. Many times a caucus will be all that is needed to move off a deadlocked point in the negotiation. If you caucus unexpectedly, the opposing party wonders why you have chosen that particular moment to have a discussion. Many deals are closed immediately following a caucus or a planned interruption, which gives both parties the time to think clearly about alternatives and potential solutions to a deadlocked point.

Your negotiation plan should provide for a minimum of three caucuses that you will take, no matter how long the negotiating session. Even in a one-on-one negotiation with a developer, it is possible to caucus by excusing yourself to visit the toilet or by excusing yourself to call the office for important messages. Develop your own technique for breaking away from the negotiation so that you can think clearly or outline to yourself the key points that have been discussed so far. If the true purpose of the negotiation is to arrive at an agreement, do not allow yourself to regret having agreed to something without thinking it through clearly by taking advantage of a few minutes during a negotiation to examine the advantages and disadvantages of an agreement under current circumstances.

Logistics Make a Difference

Because logistics play such an important part in the negotiation of a contract, it is vitally important that your staff research and plan the entire logistical approach to the negotiation session. Although this may be nearly impossible in a one-on-one negotiation, it is still possible to anticipate a series of conditions under which logistical considerations can be considered. For instance, if you are aware that a developer client always meets at the same restaurant, you can reserve a specific table for your next meeting, tipping the maître d' accordingly so that you have control of the logistical circumstances of the meeting. Doing so may provide you just the edge necessary to assure a win-win solution in the next win-lose circumstance. Also remember that the five senses are important in logistical considerations. The comfort level of all parties is affected by each of the senses. Plan the logistical implications of each body sense on the particular negotiation. Do not take logistics lightly. They alone could make the difference between winning and losing at your next negotiation.

5 The Six-Step Timing Strategy

- What is most important when negotiating a design contract?

- How fine should you break down your scope definitions?

- What if a client asks for a price right away?

- At what point should you be willing to quote a price?

- How do you know that your price is appropriate?

- What if the client cannot define scope but still wants a price?

One of the biggest problems faced by design professionals when negotiating a design contract is to pace the negotiation so that each logical step of your plan is executed prior to moving to the next step. This chapter introduces you to a six-step strategy that will help your team achieve your objectives. Follow this strategy even when a client poses an impossible ultimatum to you.

Pay careful attention to the order of the steps. The order has a purpose and each step must be complete before proceeding to the next step. If you cannot reach agreement on any one of the steps, stop the negotiation and caucus until an agreement can be reached. By moving on to another step prior to completing one, you defeat the entire purpose of this strategy.

Step 1: Define Project Scope

One of the most difficult aspects of any negotiation, especially a price-sensitive negotiation, is the necessity to define precisely and accurately the scope of work prior to committing to a price. Whenever we discuss the issue of scope with design professionals, it is clear that the accuracy of scope is most often the stumbling block encountered during a poor negotiation. For instance, one of the most common problem areas with scope in today's world is encountered when design professionals are asked for fee bids. Most clients simply ask you for your price on a typical building or a typical study without defining the specifics of their program or their requirements for the project. Quoting a price under these circumstances is suicidal. Without scope definition that reflects the problems of the particular project, it is impossible to quote an accurate or meaningful price to a client.

Therefore, step one in our six-step strategy for timing the negotiation is to define accurately the scope of work. Use all your resources to do so. During past years your experience has given you a wealth of data that you can now draw upon to ask questions of your client prior to defining scope. Set forth what will be done precisely and what the expectations of the client are in each part of the scope. Whether you use standard American Institute of Architects (AIA) phase definitions or whether you use any other segmented approach to project definition, it is wise to break down your project into bite-sized pieces so that the accuracy of the scope can be improved. We recommend that you define your scope in no fewer than 20 segments and that any segment that is larger than 5 percent of the total project be further subdivided for definition.

Step 2: Set Project Schedule

Unfortunately, after most design professionals have defined the scope of a project, they next respond quickly with a price. However, there are several other elements that affect the price and all of them render meaningless any price given at the end of scope definition alone. The first of these items is the schedule for the project. It is well known that there is a significant impact on your price depending on how the schedule for your design work and for the construction of the project will be handled.

Generally, shorter projects are more profitable to design firms. For this reason, specify a precise schedule with your client, demonstrating the exact timing of each element of the scope. If you have done your job well in defining your scope, the further definition of schedule that is required here should be an easy task. Again, you may find out by defining the schedule that your scope is not as accurate as it should be, and you may want to return to scope definition to clarify items within it that are not clear. All of this should be done before you quote a price. However, after you have quoted a price, it is very difficult to negotiate scope or schedule changes that raise the price for your client.

Types of Schedules. When defining schedule, try to use a simple and straightforward scheduling method that allows the client to understand completely what you are saying. Two of the simplest and most recognizable types of schedules are defined below:

❶ *Milestone Charts*. Perhaps the simplest scheduling method is the milestone chart. In its most basic form, this method consists of identifying the target completion date for each activity in the schedule. Additional information that can be added to a milestone chart includes the actual completion date and name of the person responsible for performing each task. The major advantages of milestone charts are their ease of preparation and emphasis on target completion dates.

The best applications for milestone charts are short projects with few participants and little interrelationship between activities. Probably the most common example of such projects is the preparation of proposals, as in Figure 5-1. Another good application for milestone charts is for summarizing complex schedules containing many tasks. When doing so, list only key activities to avoid excessive detail, which can defeat the purpose of the chart. An example of this type of milestone chart is the report preparation schedule form presented in Figure 5-2.

A major drawback of the milestone chart is that it shows *only* completion dates. For complex projects,

● **Figure 5-1. Milestone Chart for a Typical Proposal**

Activity Description	Responsibility	Target Date	Completed
1. Proposal cover	DB	3/16/81	✔
2. Letter of transmittal	AWL	3/27/81	
3. Introduction	AWL	3/27/81	
4. Scope of services	MRH	3/22/81	✔
5. Project schedule	MRH	3/25/81	✔
6. Project budget	MRH	3/25/81	✔
7. Project organization	DB	3/25/81	✔
8. Appendix A. Qualifications	DB	3/24/81	
9. Appendix B. Biographical data	DB	3/26/81	✔
10. Typing and graphics	DB	3/30/81	
11. Final editing	AWL	4/1/81	
12. Printing, binding, and mailing	DB	4/3/81	

● Figure 5-2. Report Preparation Schedule

Job Name *Ft. Cannon Warehouse*   Date ___4/6/81___

Job Number ___2264___   Project Manager *D. Burstein*

	Date	To be reviewed/ approved by:
1. Complete detailed work plan	4/15/81	MRH
2. Complete general outline of report	4/20/81	MRH
3. Complete detailed outline of report with lists of tables and figures	4/28/81	MRH
4. Interim submittals to client	5/14/81	MRH, AWL
	6/1/81	MRH, AWL
5. Complete first draft of report	7/1/81	MRH, AWL
6. Complete drafts of figures	7/1/81	MRH, AWL
7. Complete editing of report	7/21/81	AWL
8. Complete final draft of report	7/24/81	AWL
9. Submit draft report to client	8/1/81	AWL
10. Receive comments from client	8/15/81	
11. Submit final report to client	9/1/81	AWL

Draft typing to be done by   HHH, JW, RNP

Editing to be done by   LTP

Final typing to be done by   HHH, JW

Graphics to be done by   VAJ, VMT

this may result in uncertainty about when each activity should begin, as illustrated in the milestone chart in Figure 5-3. Although the tasks are listed in the general order in which they are to be done, there is much overlapping of completion dates. Furthermore, comparing the actual completion dates with the target dates provides only a general indication of the overall schedule status. This project is clearly too complex to be adequately controlled using a milestone chart.

❷ *Bar Charts.* Some of the drawbacks of milestone charts can be overcome by using a slightly more complex method—the bar chart (also known as the Gantt chart). Probably the most widely used planning tool among design professionals, a bar chart consists of a list of tasks presented along the left side of a page with horizontal bars along the right side indicating the scheduled start and finish dates for each task. A bar chart for the project shown in Figure 5-3 is presented in Figure 5-4.

The biggest drawbacks of bar charts are that they do not show the interrelationship among various tasks, nor indicate which activities are most crucial for completing the entire project on schedule. As a result, some activities may inadvertently be omitted from the original project schedule, only to be discovered when it is too late. Also, assigning equal importance to each activity (implicit in the bar chart method) may leave you in a quandary if you are forced to decide which task should be delayed in the event of a manpower shortage. This confusion may result in assigning top priorities to the wrong tasks.

Despite these drawbacks, bar charts remain an effective method of controlling projects with total fees in the $50,000 to $2,000,000 range.

No single scheduling method is applicable for all projects. Figure 5-5 summarizes some of the most important criteria for selecting the best scheduling method. Review these criteria for each specific project and then select the scheduling method that is best suited to the criteria with the highest priorities prior to planning your negotiation.

● Figure 5-3. Milestone Chart for Sample Project

Project Activity	Responsibility	Target Date	Actual Date
A. Develop background data	PJS	5/1/84	9/12/84
B1. Select case study sites	BEB	4/1/83	3/22/83
B2. Prepare briefing documents	DSF	2/1/83	3/6/83
B3. Develop data management plan	DSF	4/1/83	3/22/83
B4. Visit case study sites	DSF/WEW	10/1/83	9/26/83
B5. Analyze waste samples	WGC	12/1/83	
C1. Develop computer cost models	DSF	4/1/82	6/12/82
C2. Perform preliminary case study designs	FRT	12/1/82	
C3. Estimate case study disposal costs	FRT	1/1/83	
D. Evaluate treatment, recovery, reuse	WEW	6/1/83	
E. Assess cost impacts	JAW	9/1/82	
F. Evaluate cost impact models	DSF/JAW	6/1/82	
G1a. Prepare background data report	PJS	8/1/83	
G1b. Prepare site visit report	DSF	12/1/83	
G1c. Prepare sampling/analysis report	WGC	2/1/84	
G2. Prepare draft report	DB	6/1/84	
G3. Prepare final report	DB	8/1/84	
H. Project management	DB	6/1/82	

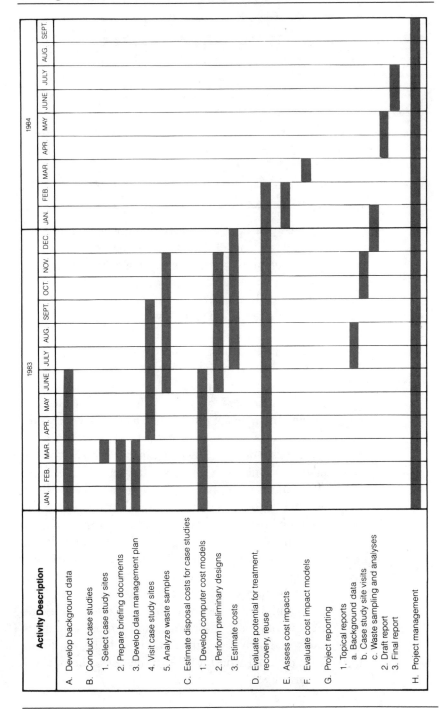

Figure 5-5. Criteria for Selecting the Proper Scheduling Method

Evaluation Criteria	Milestone	Bar Chart	CPM Diagram	Full Wall Schedule
1. Ease of communication	Good	Good	Poor	Excellent
2. Cost to prepare	Minimal	Minimal	Extensive	Moderate
3. Cost to update	Minimal	Minimal	Extensive	Moderate
4. Degree of control	Fair	Good	Excellent	Good
5. Applicability to large projects	Poor	Fair	Excellent	Good
6. Applicability to small projects	Excellent	Good	Poor	Good
7. Commitment from project team	Fair	Fair	Fair	Excellent
8. Client appeal	Fair	Good	Excellent	Excellent

Once you have described a complete and accurate schedule to your client, the client will often ask for a price. Again we recommend that you not quote a price yet, since you have completed only two steps in the six-step timing strategy. Instead, resist the temptation to quote a price and move on to the next step.

Step 3: Identify the Project Team

One of the most important aspects of any negotiation is to identify the people who will work on the project. Prior to quoting any price on a project, identify specific members of your design team as well as specific members of other teams who will work on the project. It is easy to see that a team made up of all principals would produce significantly higher billing rates than one made up of all draftspeople. Yet, time after time, we see design firms quoting fees to clients without taking into consideration the exact identity of the individuals who will work on the project. Assemble your team as much as possible by name. If you have done your job in steps 1 and 2 of the six-step timing strategy, you should be able to identify precisely the hours and the people necessary to work on the team. Remember also that it is often more efficient to have a high-priced team member who accurately performs a specified task than to have a junior team member who must learn the task as he or she is performing it.

Another important factor when finalizing the team is to consider any consultants in the design work. It is not enough to identify the firm that you are quoting as a consultant. Instead, always try to identify the specific members of the consultant's team as well as your own.

Man-Hour Estimates. It is now time to develop man-hour estimates for each member of the team. Note that you are not yet ready to show these estimates to your client. More importantly, it is your job to begin identifying specific numbers of hours and the specific tasks that each person on your team will complete within the scope and schedule outlined in steps 1 and 2. Figure 5-6 demonstrates a typical man-hour estimate that has been calculated to show individuals who will perform specific tasks on an upcoming design project. Use it as an example to create your own man-hour estimate, and most importantly, remember that this is only an estimate and not an accurate reflection of what will actually be written in the final contract. Figure 5-7 lists the basic tasks needed by you in the scheduling process; it is keyed to the tasks listed in Figure 5-6.

Step 4: Define Work Quality

One of the least discussed terms in design firm negotiations is the quality of design work. Perhaps it is because the subjectivity of design quality is difficult to discuss with a client. Or perhaps it is because clients assume that all design work will be "Taj Mahal" quality and that design professionals must outperform their prior award-winning project on every job. In any case, discussing the subjective factor of design quality, although it is difficult, is one of the most important tasks that you can perform prior to finalizing your price negotiations on a project. Set objective criteria for the subjective quality of the design. For instance, when looking at design quality offer three design alternatives that you will research for the design. Our preference is to specify an exact quantity of design alternatives to research as the easiest way to objectively

● Figure 5-6. Project Estimating Sheet

Prepared by DB Date 11/26/79 Project Example Number ____ Client DOE

Category of Personnel / Rate per Hour

Phase/task	Principal $22/hr (hrs / $)	Proj Mgr $16/hr	Arch/Eng $13/hr	Technician $10/hr	Drafting $8/hr	Secretary $6/hr	B DIRECT LABOR COSTS	C OVERHEAD (B×1.5)	D OTHER DIRECT COSTS	E EST COST B+C+D	F CONTIN- GENCES	G TOTAL BUDGET (E+F)	H PROFIT	I PROJECT VALUE (G+H)
A	20 / 440	20 / 320	200 / 2600	40 / 400	40 / 320	20 / 120	340 / 4200	6,300	2640	13,140	1,314	14,454	1,445	15,899
B1	8 / 176	16 / 256	40 / 520	0 / 0	0 / 0	8 / 48	72 / 1000	1,500	410	2,920	292	3,212	321	3,533
B2	0 / 0	20 / 320	40 / 520	0 / 0	20 / 160	20 / 120	100 / 1120	1,680	160	2,960	296	3,256	326	3,582
B3	12 / 264	40 / 640	120 / 1560	0 / 0	20 / 160	40 / 240	232 / 2864	4,296	490	7,650	765	8,415	842	9,257
B4	20 / 440	60 / 960	400 / 5200	0 / 0	0 / 0	0 / 0	480 / 6600	9,900	3,200	19,700	1,970	21,670	2,167	23,837
B5	20 / 440	20 / 320	40 / 520	400 / 4000	0 / 0	40 / 240	500 / 5080	7,620	4,800	17,500	1,750	19,250	1,925	21,175
C1	8 / 176	20 / 320	120 / 1560	60 / 600	20 / 160	40 / 240	268 / 3056	4,584	420	8,060	806	8,866	887	9,753
C2	20 / 440	40 / 640	160 / 2080	0 / 0	120 / 960	20 / 120	360 / 4240	6,360	260	10,860	1,086	11,946	1,195	13,141
C3	8 / 176	20 / 320	160 / 2080	80 / 800	0 / 0	12 / 72	280 / 3448	5,172	200	8,820	882	9,702	970	10,672
D	8 / 176	12 / 192	80 / 1040	0 / 0	20 / 160	20 / 120	140 / 1688	2,532	200	4,420	442	4,862	486	5,348
E	20 / 440	60 / 960	40 / 520	0 / 0	0 / 0	12 / 72	132 / 1992	2,988	280	5,260	526	5,786	579	6,365
F	20 / 440	40 / 640	80 / 1040	0 / 0	12 / 96	12 / 72	164 / 2288	3,432	520	6,240	624	6,864	686	7,550
G1a	8 / 176	20 / 320	80 / 1040	20 / 200	80 / 640	120 / 720	328 / 3096	4,644	1,200	8,940	894	9,834	983	10,817
G1b	8 / 176	20 / 320	80 / 1040	20 / 200	80 / 640	120 / 720	328 / 3096	4,644	1,200	8,940	894	9,834	983	10,817
G1c	8 / 176	20 / 320	80 / 1040	20 / 200	80 / 640	120 / 720	328 / 3096	4,644	1,200	8,940	894	9,834	983	10,817
G2	20 / 440	80 / 1280	160 / 2080	80 / 800	120 / 960	240 / 1440	700 / 7000	10,500	600	18,100	1,810	19,910	1,991	21,901
G3	8 / 176	40 / 640	40 / 520	20 / 200	20 / 160	60 / 360	188 / 2056	3,084	2,800	7,940	794	8,734	873	9,607
H	60 / 1320	40 / 640	40 / 520	200 / 2000	20 / 160	40 / 240	205 / 4800	7,200	1,400	13,400	1,340	14,740	1,474	16,214
TOTALS	256 / $5632	708 / 11,328	1960 / 25,480	740 / 7400	652 / 5216	944 / 5664	5260 / $60,720	91,080	21,990	173,790	17,379	191,169	19,116	210,285

A.	Develop Background Data
B1.	Select Case Study Sites
B2.	Prepare Briefing Documents
B3.	Develop Data Management Plan
B4.	Visit Case Study Sites
B5.	Analyze Waste Samples
C1.	Develop Computer Cost Models
C2.	Perform Preliminary Case Study Site Designs
C3.	Estimate Case Study Disposal Costs
D.	Evaluate Potential for Treatment, Recovery, Reuse
E.	Assess Cost Impacts
F.	Evaluate Cost Impacts Models
G1a.	Prepare Background Data Report
G1b.	Prepare Site Visit Report
G1c.	Prepare Sampling and Analyses Report
G2.	Prepare Draft Report
G3.	Prepare Final Report
H.	Project Management

treat the issue of design work quality. Whenever you define design alternatives by a specific number, it is clear that any additional number must be paid for by the client. You could also specify that the project must win a design award as part of your contract.

Whenever you leave design quality as a subjective and undefined aspect of a contract, it can only lead to disaster later on. One item that you never want to put in this part of your contract is that "the project must be approved by the executive committee." Such a statement leaves you wide open to contract disputes later in the project.

Step 5: Discuss Project Risk/Profit

Risk is hardly ever discussed in a design negotiation. Perhaps it is fear on the part of design professionals that the client may reject the firm that raises the risks involved in the project. However, without discussing risk with the client, you should brainstorm about the risks involved within your firm prior to quoting a price. There are several risks that can be encountered in taking on a new project. For instance:

❶ The project could use all your available manpower, meaning that you would have to turn down a future project that could provide a higher profit level than the one you are negotiating.

❷ There could be technical risks on the project that you have not encountered as a design professional. Perhaps you are designing a nuclear power plant, or a new earthen dam, or even a simple retaining wall on which you have had no prior experience. Your technical risk may be enhanced by the fact that junior professionals will work on the project to keep the fees low. In such instances liability and technical risk should always be discussed before quoting a price.

❸ Competition might be kept busy with the project. There is always the risk that if you take on a difficult project, it may be a sufficient burden to your firm to keep you out of the marketplace, allowing the competition to take advantage of your burden with this client. One discussion that should always occur is the risk of allowing a project to be taken by your competition so that they will be kept busy and out of the way during future design firm selections.

❹ One of the risks always considered is the financial risk on the project. Perhaps there is a major element of the project that you have not clearly defined in the scope or in the schedule which will present a significant risk to you if you take on the project. Changes in scope are one such risk. Have you defined your change procedure well enough with the clients so that you can avoid the risk of undertaking a major change without being paid for it?

Once you have discussed fully the risks involved in the project, it is time to assign a profit figure to it. Remember that it is not unreasonable for you to earn as much as 50 percent profit on a project that entails significant risk and that will tie up manpower for a significant amount of time. Do not be trapped by allowing yourself to believe that 15 percent is a reasonable profit on a design project. Remember that profit must cover firmwide overhead and operating expenses above and beyond the project profit itself. Also remember that there is a risk/reward balance on the profit scale. If you are assuming large risks, your profit should be equally large. If you are assuming small risks, your profits should be equally small. The amount of your profit should be kept as secret as possible from your client, since it is one of the trump cards that you can use at the negotiating table. Unfortunately, with government negotiators, there are profit limits set on the amount of profit that you are allowed within a project. (We will discuss this problem in Chapter 14.)

Step 6:
Quote a Price

Now that you have successfully covered and agreed upon the scope, schedule, team, work quality, and risk factors involved in the project, it is time to quote the price. Never quote a price prior to fully understanding and agreeing upon all five prior items in this list. Then when you quote a price, remember the importance of the value versus cost analysis.

During the past 50 years, design professionals have been subconsciously trained to think in "cost plus" terms. Ask yourself how often you consider the number of man-hours and simply add a profit to those man-hours to arrive at a price. Also, ask yourself how often you use a fee schedule as a reminder to check your price. How often have you totaled all your costs, only to add a "reasonable profit of 15 percent" on it to arrive at a price? We suggest that you throw out all these ideas and instead think in terms of the value of the project to your client.

Have you ever taken a client to lunch and saved the client $50,000 or more by recommending that they not purchase a site for development? Unlike other professionals, it is sometimes difficult for us as design professionals to think in terms of value instead of in terms of cost. To think in terms of value, assemble all total lifetime project costs including design, construction, and maintenance for the project over a 10- to 20-year period prior to quoting your design fee. How does what you will quote as a price compare with the total dollars that will be spent by the client during the entire life of the project? Perhaps by making a very small decision within the design phase of the project, you could save the client millions of dollars. If you are in a position to make such a decision, should you quote a price based on cost and cost alone, or should your price reflect more of your true value as a design professional?

Value-oriented pricing is an important subject in the negotiation process. Tied to it is the format of your contract, which we recommend should always be a lump sum if you are quoting a value-oriented price.

If you have done your homework well and have agreed upon the five steps mentioned earlier, quote your price in bite-sized pieces relative to the scope. Depending on the negotiating setting, it may even be wise never to quote the total price for the entire project, but only to give prices as they relate to each scope item. By quoting a price in this manner, your client can pick and choose from a menu of scope items that they may or may not elect to include. Likewise, this method allows you to defend your price by taking out of the scope any items not desired by the client. It is impossible to negotiate price unless you have defined scope, schedule, team, work quality, and risk. Doing so can only lead you to reduce your price without reducing the amount of work necessary to perform the project. After all, if you are discussing a price on a project prior to discussing any of the other items, you are operating in a vacuum.

Reimbursables. The discussion concerning value versus cost applies equally to reimbursable expenses, which should always be quoted on a unit price or value basis. Never quote a cost plus 10 percent price. This only forces you to justify forever the cost, for instance, that you are paying for one sheet of copy paper. Instead, quote a unit price per copy, per telephone unit, or per site visit for all items that you include within reimbursable expenses. The ultimate irony is that many firms are still reimbursed for blueprinting on a price per square inch, which requires bookkeepers and design professionals to measure every square inch of a blueprint and then charge on a two or three cent per square inch basis for every print made. Often bookkeepers or accountants spend their entire week calculating a reimbursable bill that only returns to the firm the cost of such printing, without reflecting any of the risk involved for bad debts or the cost of the accountant's time in calculating all these numbers.

Value pricing is a concept that applies both to reimbursable and to professional fees. Consider how attorneys use value pricing when they charge for wills at a rate of $300 to $500 apiece. The will is taken off a word processor in most cases and modified slightly in 15 to 30 minutes by the attorney. It is then reprocessed and mailed to you together with an invoice for $500. In the design professions, we prepare specifications and over 90 percent of all firms charge only by the hour for the word processing operator who runs off the specifications. Instead, we should be charging for the *value* of those specifications to our client, which would produce a much higher profitability for a document that contains the potential of significant risk to our professional status.

Have Patience with All Six Steps

The next time you are faced with a client who demands the price on a project prior to defining scope, present them with the six-step negotiating strategy. Ask the client to clearly define the scope and spend as much time as necessary defining that scope prior to moving on to step 2. Be certain you explore and explore and explore, even if hours must be invested in the definition of scope prior to moving on to the schedule. Likewise, invest an equal number of hours negotiating the specifics of schedule, team, work quality, and risk prior to quoting a price. Whenever the client asks for a price, postpone answering until all other items are clearly understood by both you and the client. Investing this amount of time in a negotiating process leads to a win-win agreement. If you have chosen any other strategy, you may wish to modify the approach, and in fact, if you have chosen a win-lose strategy, you may reverse the entire approach by asking for price first and everything else next.

Finally, do not forget the importance of value

pricing versus cost pricing as an element in your price quote. Whenever possible, do not reveal your cost to your client, but instead quote a price that reflects the value of what will be accomplished in the work. Although it is difficult and takes much time to get used to, the future profitability of the design professions rests with each one of us quoting value prices to our clients and eliminating the concept of "cost plus" from our vocabulary. Without such strategies, productivity improvement tools such as computer-aided drafting equipment only lead us to quote fewer and fewer hours at lower and lower rates to our clients while we perform more and more work of greater value for them. This six-step timing strategy is perhaps the most important element within the entire concept of negotiating. Practice it routinely.

Part 2

At the Negotiating Table

Now that you are prepared with a plan, it is time to put it into action. This part will focus on the specific circumstances you will encounter as you negotiate, including such varied concerns as dress, logistics, and objections that you must overcome.

6 At the Bargaining Table

- When should you arrive at a negotiation?

- How does dress affect the outcome?

- How long should you plan to stay at the negotiating table?

- How should you start the session?

- How should you use cost data most effectively?

- What about using outside surveys to support your own numbers?

- How can you time your concessions to assure that you also get what you want?

negotiation is much like a presentation. Most often the design professional travels to the site of the client to sit in a conference-style setting and conduct the negotiation. Of course, there are a wide variety of circumstances that create different environments. However, negotiating most design firm contracts requires that several parties sit around a table to discuss the specifics of the project and to arrive at a price. This chapter deals with a variety of subjects, all of which focus on the negotiating session itself. Included within the chapter are discussions on when to arrive, how to dress, how to open, how to use cost data, how and when to caucus, how to use emotion effectively, and how to time concessions precisely. Use this chapter as a checklist to examine how you performed on your last negotiation and as a planning tool to cover the vital elements for your next one.

When to Arrive

As with marketing presentations, it is important to arrive early at a negotiation session. Make sure you allow plenty of time for travel in case you miss a train or get stuck in traffic. In addition, when you arrive early, you have time to think through the negotiating process in a relaxed atmosphere.

One of the most significant benefits of arriving early—getting a feel for the situation—can be shown in the following example: A design professional attending one of our negotiating seminars told us of a presentation at which he planned to overcome a significant geographic objection from a client by using the train between their Pennsylvania office and the Washington, D.C., client's office. When the design team arrived early on site, they were seated next to the client's secretary, who informed them that the client's daughter had lost her pet dog of 12 years the evening before. It was killed by a freight train passing behind their house. The design team immediately restructured its presentation to eliminate any reference to trains and was able to be successful in achieving the selection and contract for the project. Of course, there is nothing to say that the firm would not have been chosen anyway. However, there is also no reason to rub salt in a wound if you are able to find out significant information by arriving early for the negotiation session.

Arriving early also expresses your interest and eagerness to work with the client. Let them see that you want the project and that you want to have a beneficial relationship once the negotiation has finished.

How to Dress   When giving design firm presentations, we recommend that you dress so that your clothing is not noticed by the client. Simply stated, this means that you appear neither over dressed nor under dressed for the particular situation. Dressing to be "not noticed" requires you to identify exactly how the client expects a design professional to dress.

When negotiating, however, the opposite is true. In negotiating, you should always wear attire that marks you as a person in a position of power. Men should wear dark three-piece suits with shiny black shoes, neatly groomed hair, and jewelry appropriate to authority. Eliminate calculator watches, leisure suits, and unshaven beards or uncut hair. Women should be smartly dressed in a business suit with a high collar, which reflects professionalism and dignity.

First impressions are important when negotiating, and people like to deal with people who are successful. For this reason, it is not bad to wear expensive jewelry or expensive clothing when you enter the negotiating room. Remember that it is easier to remove your sportcoat or suit jacket, if that seems appropriate, than it is to create an entirely different image on the spot. Always dress in a businesslike and respectful manner, but as we have said, dress for power when entering the negotiation session.

If you do not believe this recommendation, put on a pair of blue jeans and a sweatshirt and walk into the nearest branch of your local bank to apply for a loan. Carefully record how you are treated by the people in the bank, especially people who don't know who you are. Now, go into another bank dressed in a three-piece suit or a well-tailored business suit and see if your reception is any different.

There is no doubt that the way you are dressed sets a style for the entire negotiation session. When you are attempting to conduct a win-win strategy within your negotiation, it is important that your dress be as powerful as you need to set up your strategy. Of course, if you have chosen a lose-lose or a lose-win strategy, you may wish to wear blue jeans to the next negotiation session.

How to Open

One of the most awkward times in any negotiation is the opening of the session itself. The following are some recommendations to help you get more comfortable with the entire negotiation setting:

1 Rearrange the seating. If you have done your homework in preparing for the negotiation, you may decide that rearranging the seating is appropriate as an opening tactic. By rearranging the seating you are taking the focus of your client's attention off you and placing it upon the logistics of the situation. Likewise, by your physical activity, you will arouse small conversations with those from the client group. Often these small conversations are all that it takes to help both sides of the negotiation feel comfortable with one another.

2 Set up cards for names. If you decide not to change the entire physical setup of the negotiation, consider using hand-written tent cards to identify each of the people in the session. You can place those cards in front of each individual. Doing so gives you the opportunity to shake each person's hand and to let each one know that you are an active "take control" person in the negotiation process.

3 Ask for the telephone and make a call. Asking for the telephone is a sign that you are not timid about your upcoming meeting. Make an important call that can be overheard, and be certain to leave the number where you can be reached. Doing so sets up a perfect opportunity for a later interruption, which works to your benefit by allowing you to either take or reject the call when it comes. The act of asking for a telephone and making a call implies to the client that you are busy. It also shows that you have other business that is equally as important to you as their contract. Remember that people like to deal with successful people, so by asking to make a call you are not insulting them.

❹ Be straightforward. We often forget to be ourselves when walking into a meeting. Remember that clients are people too, and they have human feelings and apprehensions just as you do. Walk up to the client. Introduce yourself. Be cordial, and tell them what a pleasure it is that you are here to negotiate the final contract for their upcoming project. Doing so sets a professional tone in the meeting, and it allows you to get on with the meeting without further delay.

One of the most important rules in a negotiation session is never to open the meeting with humor. Telling a joke or opening the meeting with a whimsical comment puts you in a position of weakness in the eyes of your client. Remember that you are attempting to establish a position of strength from which to negotiate a businesslike agreement. Humor has no place at the beginning of a negotiation, even though it has a very good place later on.

Use of Cost Data

One of the most powerful tools in a negotiation is the use of external cost data to support your own numbers. Be prepared at every negotiation session to have available a directory or a survey that reinforces all the numbers you quote in your price. Although this is especially true with government negotiations, there are many private clients who are now using third-party surveys to justify their hiring of design firms. Obtain as many surveys as possible and have a library full of data to support your own cost information when negotiating with a client. Remember that your own cost estimates can be questioned continually. Most numbers can be made to look as positive or negative as need be by the right accountant. Only through the use of independent published cost data can you reinforce your figures with a significant amount of credibility. Tables 6-1 and 6-2 show typical pages found in the

Table 6-1. Overhead Comparison between Design Firms*

	Overhead Rate (before profit distribution)		Overhead Rate (after profit distribution)		Labor Overhead (based on direct labor)		G & A Overhead (based on direct labor)	
	Mean, %	Median, %	Mean, %	Median, %	Mean, %	Median, %	Mean, %	Median, %
Overall	143.6	148.6	172.4	161.1	43.3	42.0	112.1	110.7
Staff: 1–20	152.3	171.8	176.7	177.4	40.5	40.9	123.1	122.9
21–50	141.7	142.8	167.7	160.1	44.4	45.5	109.4	106.5
51–100	141.8	150.1	177.1	156.3	43.7	43.6	111.6	108.9
101–200	141.2	147.0	159.0	158.6	43.0	44.1	109.1	105.6
201–350	153.7	148.8	172.4	157.1	46.0	42.1	120.5	111.1
351–500	147.7	139.9	190.3	153.5	43.8	40.1	112.7	104.3
Over 500	136.7	129.4	143.6	135.2	41.6	40.3	101.8	99.1
Architectural	153.2	158.9	184.0	172.5	41.7	43.6	121.8	128.6
Engineering	140.6	148.4	160.0	153.9	44.4	45.3	108.7	107.9
A/E	139.5	139.8	156.6	153.8	41.2	40.0	106.7	104.0
A/E/P	143.2	143.5	183.6	161.1	42.0	41.9	110.6	111.4
Other	141.3	146.2	163.8	158.6	45.2	44.0	112.5	107.9
All U.S.	146.3	150.3	174.0	159.3	44.1	44.3	115.5	114.2
Northeast	145.1	148.0	161.1	162.2	44.4	43.8	105.3	104.8
South	138.3	140.8	160.7	159.7	43.6	41.1	112.3	104.3
Midwest	149.1	152.0	175.3	161.9	43.5	42.1	115.1	113.2
Southwest	128.3	120.2	152.5	146.8	42.1	39.3	101.1	89.3
West	152.7	150.8	184.7	169.4	44.0	45.8	118.6	119.2
Private	144.0	149.9	174.2	166.5	43.3	43.5	112.0	107.9
Government	144.4	147.3	171.3	158.5	43.3	43.8	109.8	108.1
Mixed	142.4	145.9	156.2	157.6	43.3	42.9	114.2	113.0

*1984 PSMJ Financial Statistics Survey.

● Table 6-2. Profit Comparisons between Design Firms*

	Net Profit before Profit Distributions and Taxes (gross revenue)		Net Profit before Profit Distributions and Taxes (net revenue)		Net Profit before Taxes (gross revenue)		Net Profit before Taxes (net revenue)	
	Mean, %	Median, %	Mean, %	Median, %	Mean, %	Median, %	Mean, %	Median, %
Overall	4.98	6.02	6.05	7.38	1.75	2.61	2.10	3.25
Staff: 1–20	(.52)	5.07	(.48)	6.67	(2.16)	2.76	(2.60)	3.61
21–50	5.72	6.45	6.82	8.39	1.58	1.00	1.77	1.30
51–100	7.00	6.29	8.41	8.29	4.10	2.96	4.89	3.54
101–200	5.91	5.45	7.19	6.78	1.74	1.98	2.19	2.26
201–350	3.55	4.56	3.83	5.59	.64	1.74	.36	2.07
351–500	4.08	4.06	5.13	5.83	1.27	1.83	1.67	2.32
Over 500	6.47	6.37	8.73	8.45	4.75	4.17	6.48	5.02
Architectural	5.61	6.44	7.81	9.36	2.04	2.09	2.67	2.92
Engineering	4.67	5.46	5.68	6.78	1.33	2.34	1.79	2.91
A/E	4.37	5.91	4.73	6.90	1.78	2.55	1.68	2.85
A/E/P	4.15	4.30	4.95	5.22	.71	1.48	.82	1.77
Other	5.54	7.05	6.35	8.56	2.45	2.90	2.76	3.24
All U.S.	3.98	5.49	5.25	6.81	1.80	3.00	2.47	3.72
Northeast	6.16	7.40	7.27	8.22	2.33	2.00	2.65	2.26
South	8.57	8.11	9.83	9.62	4.50	3.08	5.01	3.49
Midwest	2.11	3.42	2.43	4.52	(.44)	1.26	(.69)	1.51
Southwest	11.10	7.36	13.51	8.57	6.27	4.47	7.46	5.11
West	4.65	5.46	6.27	6.96	1.20	1.72	1.87	2.04
Private	4.86	6.09	5.89	7.48	1.35	2.34	1.46	2.91
Government	6.05	6.87	7.33	8.26	3.06	2.97	3.75	3.53
Mixed	4.22	5.22	5.16	6.34	1.18	2.50	1.56	3.00

( ) = loss   *1984 PSMJ Financial Statistics Survey.

Table 6-2. Continued

	Net Profit (gross revenues)		Net Profit (net revenues)		Contribution Rate (gross profit)		Net Multiplier	
	Mean, %	Median, %	Mean, %	Median, %	Mean, %	Median, %	Mean, %	Median, %
Overall	1.08	1.79	1.27	2.20	49.3	50.1	2.59	2.74
Staff: 1–20	(2.89)	1.85	(3.50)	2.71	47.3	48.6	2.85	2.75
21–50	1.18	.83	1.21	1.04	49.8	49.1	2.85	2.74
51–100	3.29	2.43	4.00	3.00	50.4	51.5	2.75	2.76
101–200	1.05	.98	1.34	1.31	51.2	52.3	2.72	2.69
201–350	.67	1.35	.62	1.51	49.5	51.1	2.80	2.69
351–500	.92	1.62	1.12	1.99	48.3	47.7	2.95	2.59
Over 500	2.68	2.30	3.63	2.68	43.0	45.2	2.60	2.53
Architectural	1.41	2.41	1.82	3.15	44.7	44.3	2.99	2.88
Engineering	.54	1.51	.82	1.95	51.6	52.3	2.78	2.73
A/E	.90	1.64	.79	2.00	49.9	50.6	2.65	2.64
A/E/P	.07	1.28	.00	1.69	48.7	48.5	2.80	2.69
Other	2.23	1.99	2.41	2.51	49.1	50.2	2.79	2.74
All U.S.	.60	2.08	.92	2.50	47.4	48.2	2.87	2.72
Northeast	1.70	1.61	1.99	1.90	50.6	51.9	2.72	2.73
South	3.34	2.59	3.71	1.86	51.0	51.4	2.81	2.69
Midwest	(.98)	1.03	(1.27)	1.19	50.3	51.2	2.69	2.69
Southwest	4.87	4.47	5.73	5.11	49.1	47.9	2.89	2.76
West	1.59	1.36	2.06	1.80	49.5	49.5	3.04	2.82
Private	.82	1.65	.78	2.17	49.4	50.1	2.90	2.76
Government	2.12	1.98	2.58	2.30	50.5	49.9	2.87	2.68
Mixed	.55	1.71	.82	2.09	48.2	50.5	2.72	2.74

( ) = loss

Professional Services Management Journal (PSMJ) Financial Statistics Survey from 1984. Such cost data provide you with a wealth of defensible information to be used in the appropriate situation within the negotiation. Appendix A contains a list of cost data available to justify a variety of expenses and labor rates in design firm negotiations.

One of the most important things to remember when using cost data is that your client has access to the very same information. Never forget that your client could use the same cost data and interpret it differently. Study cost data to determine how it was gathered and analyzed so that you completely understand the use of the numbers that you are showing to your clients. There is nothing worse than telling a client that your numbers are accurate based on the XYZ Survey only to find that the client understands that survey and how the numbers were generated better than you.

| **Use of a Caucus** | To achieve a win-win strategy, the negotiation should be extended over a long period of time. Doing so requires that several breaks be taken during a negotiation. There is always time set aside for lunch, coffee, and toilet breaks during a session. But also plan as part of your agenda to have a variety of negotiation caucuses during the meeting. The optimum and longest time that you should sit in one position is 30 minutes. After 30 minutes, fatigue sets in and the attention span of those with whom you are negotiating is significantly reduced. Several studies have shown that the actual attention span of a human being listening to a presentation is 7 to 10 seconds before the mind or eyes wander to a distraction in the room.* Because keeping the client's attention is so hard anyway, plan interruptions to allow for a smooth and comfortable transition to a workable agreement. Caucuses can be created for a variety of situations. A |

---

*Bert Decker, who is the publisher of the "Decker Communications Report," presented this material at the American Consulting Engineers Council annual convention in San Francisco on May 15, 1984.

caucus need not appear to be planned; it can also take place as the result of an interruption that was actually planned but that gives the appearance of being a normal interruption. Some of the following types of simple interruptions can facilitate caucusing:

1 Telephone calls. Establish with your secretary a pattern of telephone calls that is irregular and must be answered by you during the meeting. Remember, though, never have more than two telephone calls per day. Remember also that a telephone call allows all other parties in the room to stand and stretch for a few minutes while you respond to the call. It can also allow you to leave the room, which means that you can check on other data needed to continue negotiation.

2 Lunch breaks. Structure lunch breaks so that they occur after noontime. The most important and productive time of the day is before lunch; thus it is erroneous to schedule lunch for 11:30 A.M., thereby losing a productive hour out of your morning. Schedule a lunch break for some time between 12:30 and 1 P.M. to allow the most productive time of the morning to be extended. Also remember that the least productive time of the day is the hour immediately following lunch. For that reason schedule two or three breaks during the afternoon so that people can get up from their seats and move around.

3 Planned caucuses. It is legitimate for you to ask your client for a 15-minute break to discuss with your team several aspects of the scope or other terms of the agreement. Plan two or three caucuses within your agenda to discuss all aspects of the agreement with your own team. This may include time to make a call back to other members of the firm to get their input.

Planned breaks are one of the most effective ways to inspire the other party to arrive at an agreement or to make a concession. Whenever there is a break in the meeting, the other party has a subconscious commitment to move things along more quickly when the meeting comes back to order. The next time you are in any kind of meeting, watch what happens after a coffeebreak. Undoubtedly, because people's attention spans are brought back to life, decisions are made more quickly and agreements can be reached without the impediment of drowsiness, which is always present just before a break.

Using caucuses or interruptions in a meeting is one of the most effective tools to get your client to agree with your point of view. The timing and effective use of caucuses can be an art. The art can be studied and learned, but it requires that you practice and that you absolutely require that interruptions occur throughout the entire negotiating session. The more natural the interruptions, the less likely your client will be disturbed by the number of interruptions.

4 Toilet breaks. Of course, one of the most natural interruptions is to request a toilet break. There is no worse distraction, however, than requiring the use of toilet facilities but not asking to go. Do not be timid. Simply stop the meeting and go to the bathroom. Take as much time as necessary to stretch, rest, or make calls to get additional data for your meeting.

5 Coffeebreaks. Coffeebreaks should occur naturally in the morning and in the afternoon. If you are conducting the negotiation, schedule the coffeebreaks and inform everyone of their time prior to entering the meeting. If you are attending a negotiation in a client's office, ask what time coffee is served before starting the meeting. By doing so you are setting a time limit on the client that is subconscious and may work to your benefit.

Using Emotion Effectively

In a negotiation I participated in with a hospital client represented by the Order of the Sisters of Charity, we had arrived at a stalemate after six hours of negotiating. Our design firm negotiating team was noticeably nervous that the client would become so upset at the deadlock that they would reject our proposals for doing the project. Suddenly, the Mother Superior stood up and slammed her notebook shut looking sternly into everyone's eyes. She spoke tersely and expressed her concern with the status of the negotiations. Then, in the same stern voice, she said to everyone, "And furthermore, I must go to the bathroom to tinkle before we move on with the negotiation." Everyone in the room burst into laughter and recognized that she had used an emotional maneuver and her sense of humor to create an atmosphere that was conducive to agreement. Within five minutes after she returned to the table, we had agreed upon a contract and were able to move on to finalize all aspects of the negotiation.

Whenever you plan a negotiation, plan within your agenda a strategy that allows you to use emotion. All too often design professionals in the United States restrict themselves to unemotional and businesslike behavior in negotiating sessions. Consider how effective it is when Italians use hand gestures and loud language or when Russians hug each other freely. Think of ways to use emotion spontaneously to help break a deadlock. Use it creatively to think of ways to show that you are human, for example, through the use of natural humor.

Be extremely careful, however, that your emotion or your sense of humor does not cause an overreaction in your client and offend him or her terribly. The use of humor and of emotion is an art that must be practiced; it simply cannot be learned from a book. There are certainly individuals within your firm who use humor and emotion effectively. Do not restrict them from being part of the negotiating team. Instead, make them part of the team and instruct them that one of their most important roles is to break deadlocks through the timely use of humor or emotion.

Timing Concessions

As we have already noted, negotiators have one trait that gives them significant power when negotiating. Patience allows them to wait a long time before conceding in any negotiation. Unfortunately, American negotiators, and especially design professionals, often give up many points in a negotiation before securing anything in return for what they have given up. Timing your concessions can be one of the most important parts of your negotiating strategy. You should never give up anything unless you get something in return. Likewise, time your giveaways in the negotiation agenda so that you do not overload the front end of the negotiation session. One popular strategy is to give something that you would give anyway at the beginning of the negotiation session. Asian negotiators practice this frequently. Their philosophy is to give you something that they would have given to you anyway prior to your having to ask for it. By doing so, they set up and establish a "debt" that must be repaid by you before they will give anything else. Often, immediately after giving this "freebie," they ask for the most significant part of the agreement. Artistic as they may be, they are simply practicing the tactic of timing concessions properly.

To time concessions appropriately, draw from your list of what you want and what you are willing to give within the terms of the contract (see Chapter 10). Alternate between your strongest wants and your weakest giveaways. By doing so, you accurately space the tradeoff between what you want in the negotiation and what you are willing to give up. Whenever you lose or give away something in the negotiation, be certain to remind the client that you have just traded something for something that you want badly. Do not budge from your position until the client has given you something in return for what you have given up. We often observe design professionals who give, give, and give more, but never ask for anything in return. A negotiation is a give-and-take situation, and you should not feel obligated to give more until you have received something in return for what you have just given.

Walking Out of a Bad Session

Various aspects of the negotiation session work toward making it a success or failure. Several of the items discussed in this chapter may help to make your next negotiation a total success. But this is not always the case. Remember that each aspect of the negotiation session should be planned and that all items of the plan should be placed on an agenda that you should carry with you only for your team's use. One of the most important things to place on the agenda is your walk-out position. Remember to define precisely under what circumstances you will walk out of the negotiation. Write it on your agenda. Doing so gives you a significant amount of strength at the negotiating table. You always know what your walk-out position is, but your client does not have that knowledge.

Whenever you reach a point in the negotiation that makes it clear you will not be able to agree (that is, you have reached your walk-out position), do not hesitate to leave. It is far easier to move on to your next project with a positive feeling than it is to take on a project that is below your walk-out position.

Common Snags

- What if the client says, "You've got to do better than that"?

- How should you break a deadlock?

- What if a client says, "Take it or leave it"?

- How should you handle clients who pass on final decisions to a higher authority?

- What if the client wants you to start the project now and negotiate terms later?

- What should you do when the client expands the scope *after* the negotiation?

No matter what plan you have and no matter how good you are at establishing a strategy for negotiation, there undoubtedly comes a point in the negotiation when the client throws a series of objections at you that seem impossible to negotiate. In this chapter we examine a number of specific obstacles that have been thrown at design professionals during the last few years. These are meant to help you overcome the problems with specific win-win strategies that allow you to maintain your professionalism and not be buried by the obstacle.

Negotiating is made up of strategies, and each tactic used by a client can suggest a countertactic by your firm's team. Never allow yourself to be thrown by an obstacle without considering the offensive and defensive tactic being used by your client.

In this chapter we identify a number of objections commonly raised by clients and then give a series of suggestions for the design professional to overcome the obstacle.

Nibbling

"Nibbling" occurs after you have reached an agreement with your client. It is often introduced by the phrase, "Oh, by the way . . . we forgot to include the change that would occur on row A, column 23 on the initial structural layout as part of our original scope." After you have achieved an agreement and signed a deal, such a "nibble" could significantly undermine your financial position. Stopping such nibbling is key to your success on any project. There are four specific strategies for overcoming the problem of nibbling:

1. Quote a price immediately for the additional work scope. By quoting a price immediately, you let the client know that you have identified a nibble. Even if you are told that this particular situation is part of the scope, you still establish a precedent by letting the client know that you are watching closely all items already negotiated. You thus condition the client not to ask again.

2. Do what is asked of you and send an immediate bill for the change. This is basically the same strategy as in

step 1, but in a different form. By sending a bill you tell the client that you have identified the nibble as an extra. You also tell the client that you will not do these nibbles free of charge throughout the project.

❸ Refer to the scope of work. The two preceding suggestions are offensive strategies that show the client that you are in control of your scope of work. This suggestion is defensive. For that reason it is not as powerful as the first two, but in many cases may achieve the same result. Refer specifically to your scope of work, and ask the client exactly where the nibble is located. If you have negotiated your scope, schedule, and team appropriately as outlined in Chapter 5, you should be able to defend your position by not finding this change in your agreed-upon scope.

❹ Don't do what is asked of you. The weakest of all positions is simply to ignore the client; however, there are times when a client's nibble should be ignored, especially when you have worked with this client several times in the past and know that some of these nibbles will not result in changes later on. Thus, if you really know the client and understand that the nibble is insignificant, simply ignore it.

Escalation during the Negotiation

Escalation is similar to a nibble, only it occurs prior to achieving an agreement. For example, a client may ask you to examine only three design alternatives on a project and then throughout the negotiation refer to a fourth alternative. By implying that you will conduct four design investigations, the client has escalated the scope of work without acknowledging the fourth investigation.

Escalation most frequently occurs when there is an interruption in your negotiation overnight or for an extended period of time. When the parties resume negotiating, one or the other party may assume that they have agreed upon the escalated scope without the other party actually agreeing. To counteract escalation, use any of the following five steps:

❶ Counterescalate. When your client escalates, immediately counterescalate your price or reduce the scope of other aspects of the job to compensate for the escalation.

❷ Use peer pressure. When a client escalates a scope item and you have other design professionals or clients in the room, ask if everyone heard it that way. The use of peer pressure is very powerful, especially if anyone else disagrees with what the client has just said. Likewise, ask to see the notes of everyone or the notes of the person who is recording agreements within the session.

❸ Put the client on notice. Ask if more of this type of escalation will occur throughout the negotiation. By identifying that you are aware of the escalation, you place the client on notice that you are watching carefully all aspects of the negotiation. This earns for you the respect of the client and in most cases eliminates further escalation in the negotiation.

❹ Caucus. If you feel that the client is escalating, caucus with your team members to discuss strategy. Caucusing sets your opponents ill at ease. They wonder why you have taken a break at this particular moment. If they know they are escalating, they will recognize that you know what escalation is and are developing a strategy to counteract it. They are then placed on the defensive, and you will be on the offensive when you return from the caucus.

❺ Consider walking out. Because escalation is an unfair tactic in a win-win environment, consider a walk-out strategy under this circumstance. Before walking out at the first instance of escalation, try to use any of the preceding four strategies. However, if the escalation continues, consider walking out of the negotiation, since it may be apparent that the client will escalate continually, not only during the contract negotiation session, but after the contract has been agreed upon.

Buy Now, Negotiate Later

We have all run into clients who want to have you start immediately and negotiate later. The most common example of this is the developer who wants us to develop a set of schematic drawings so that he can get financing for a project and asks us to negotiate the deal for design fees after the financing has been granted. If you are faced with a buy-now/negotiate-later situation, use the following three strategies to place yourself in a favorable position:

❶ Set a deadline for a contract. Often the client cannot define the scope of a project and in an effort to save time does not want to go through the entire negotiating process to achieve a contract before starting the work. If this is the case, at least agree upon a calendar date by which time the contract must be set or work will stop. Do not define the cutoff in any other way than with a specific calendar date. Subjectively defining the cutoff by the "end of a phase" or by the "approval of a committee or board of directors" may mean you work on the project for months or perhaps years without ever achieving a contract. If you set a calendar date by which the contract must be achieved, you place a significant amount of pressure upon the client as that date approaches. Never work after you have established a contract date cutoff. By continuing work you place yourself in the weakest of all positions and let the client know that you are willing to work for nothing without a contract.

❷ Set a higher multiplier when you don't have a contract. One firm in the Midwest uses a rule of thumb that their multiplier on direct labor will be a 4.5 minimum whenever a contract is not negotiated and signed. Some project managers in the firm have found that over the course of a project, if the client is unwilling to negotiate a contract, their project profitability could actually go up due to client inefficiencies and lack of commitment to a contract. Of course, operating without a contract is dangerous and could lead to liability problems should you encounter a lawsuit. However, consider the advantages of operating at a higher multiplier while you define the scope necessary to achieve an equitable contract for both parties.

❸ Treat the project as an investment. Because most design professionals are not "thrown off the job" after they have begun working with a client and because the client has invested a certain amount of time transmitting project data and historic knowledge to the design team that is selected, it may work to your advantage to take a project without a contract just to get your foot in the door. Having worked on the project for a period of three to six months, you are now in a much better position to negotiate a contract with the client. After all, if you stop work or are thrown off the project, the client is forced to seek another design professional to pick up the pieces and continue the project. This alternative is not very attractive for most clients and as a result you should be in an optimum position to negotiate many of the positive terms that allow you to achieve a true win-win contract.

Escalating Authority

One of the most common mistakes made by design professionals is the failure to identify the client's proper authority before entering into a negotiation. After you have negotiated for days or weeks with a client, the client negotiating team may end by saying that all will be fine as long as "the boss" agrees with what has been negotiated. You can be certain that the boss will never agree. In such cases, you usually lose further ground in the final contract. If you are faced with this kind of escalating authority in your negotiation, use some of the following tactics when the boss does come into the negotiation after your original round:

❶ Counterescalate. If the boss immediately escalates, asking for new terms or new conditions within the contract, do not hesitate to immediately counterescalate your price. Doing so lets the higher authority know that you have been a successful negotiator in the first round and that you have already agreed upon the scope, schedule, team, quality of work, and risks prior to finalizing that round of negotiations.

❷ Don't repeat arguments. If you have won any significant terms in the initial session, do not volunteer to repeat anything agreed to in the first round. Instead, allow the client's higher authority to do all the talking. In many cases, terms you have agreed upon will stand if the higher authority does not open them up for further discussion. Thus, only deal with issues that are brought up for renegotiation by the higher authority.

3 If you have lost in the initial round of negotiating, it may be worth your while to reopen the entire negotiation session from the beginning. When you do so, be certain to bring up all aspects of the negotiation, and be willing to invest the same amount of time that it took to negotiate that first agreement. Remember that you have an agenda for the negotiation that you should return to whenever a higher authority is brought into the picture.

4 Protest. If you have negotiated in good faith and the client now brings in a higher authority that he or she has not informed you about earlier—or if the client deliberately lied and said that he or she had the authority to sign the contract—consider protesting the entire negotiation. It is unfair and perhaps unethical of one party seeking a professional contract to deceptively manipulate the other party. If a mechanism exists for a protest, use it. Otherwise consider walking out.

5 Be prepared to walk out. A walk-out is definitely an option when a higher authority is brought into the picture. To counteract the entire strategy of escalating authority, be certain that you ask at the beginning if the team members with whom you are negotiating have the authority to sign the contract. Doing so lets you know exactly what authority they have to negotiate any aspect of the contract. If they do not have the authority to sign the contract, do not give up anything significant. Trading anything at this stage of the contract without the client authority being present can only hurt you later on.

Limited Authority

When you identify that the client team has limited authority, how should you act? The clients who purposely inform you that they have limited authority are giving you an opportunity to try some of your most courageous negotiating tactics. Try the following suggestions the next time your client team has limited authority to negotiate:

1 Raise new questions. Raise questions that suggest completely new areas of service that you could negotiate into your contract. Doing so gives your client the opportunity to go back to a higher authority with more possibilities for using your services. This tactic also allows you to discuss and include more terms, even if you remove some of them from the final contract during a subsequent negotiating session with the higher authority.

2 Be courageous. Use emotion and a sense of humor freely. Remember that you may have to work with this individual as part of the client team throughout the life of the contract. Do not ever intimidate or badger a client negotiator. The use of emotion or humor can help establish good relations when dealing with a client with limited authority.

3 Make mistakes. By this we do not suggest that you give away anything, but instead that you make some obvious mistakes that can be corrected in a later negotiation with a higher authority. Attempt to set up a circumstance that will entice a higher authority to talk directly to you. This could undermine the entire agreement that you arrive at with the lower authority and allow you to completely reopen the negotiation at a later point. For instance, totally underestimate the number of man-hours necessary to prepare the drawing of details for the project. Then when you deal with the higher authority say that you misunderstood the client's requirements so a complete renegotiation is needed and thank the client for the second chance.

4 Say no graciously. If you have planned a strategy for your negotiation to deal only with the client representative who has the authority to sign the contract, learn how to say no graciously to the person with limited authority. Recognize that you may be jeopardizing the entire contract if the client insists that the limited authority must prepare the way for the higher authority in the final negotiation.

Escaping from Authority. In a situation where the client team has only limited authority, you may have to find a way to escape from your full authority to sign, using whatever tactics are available to avoid overcommiting your firm. Some of the following tactics may be useful to you:

❶ Be honest and suggest that you simply need time to think about the agreement before agreeing to it. Under a win-win strategy, honesty may be the best weapon. Suggest a one-week review of the contract so you have time to think about it. During that week you can develop a strategy for dealing with anything in the contract that you really object to.

❷ Suggest that you must check all aspects of your agreement with partners or with a committee on contracts. Doing so escalates your part of the negotiation to a higher authority. It also allows you to avoid committing immediately. Of course, it is optimum if you have established this strategy early in the negotiation by telling the client that you must check all aspects of the contract with your partner prior to signing. If you haven't already done this, it is never too late to suggest such an alternative to escape from full authority.

❸ Check with an attorney. A logical and fully justifiable method to escape from full authority is to check with your attorney before committing yourself to anything. Use this defense particularly if you are backed into a corner by a client.

❹ Check the agreement with others, such as mechanical consultants, engineers, or interior designers. Notify the client that you must check with others prior to making any final commitments under the current agreement.

❺ If it is true, suggest that agreeing to what is in the contract may violate your state's professional registration laws. Such a suggestion gives you time to investigate the registration laws and to analyze whether or not any aspects of the contract deserve review.

Beating a "Take-It-or-Leave-It" Attitude	One of the most unfortunate tactics used by clients is the handing down of an ultimatum in negotiations. The ultimatum always destroys a win-win strategy. Whenever you hear the words "take it or leave it," you

have just been placed in a win-lose circumstance by your client and you should react appropriately. Use the following suggestions to react to a take-it-or-leave-it tactic:

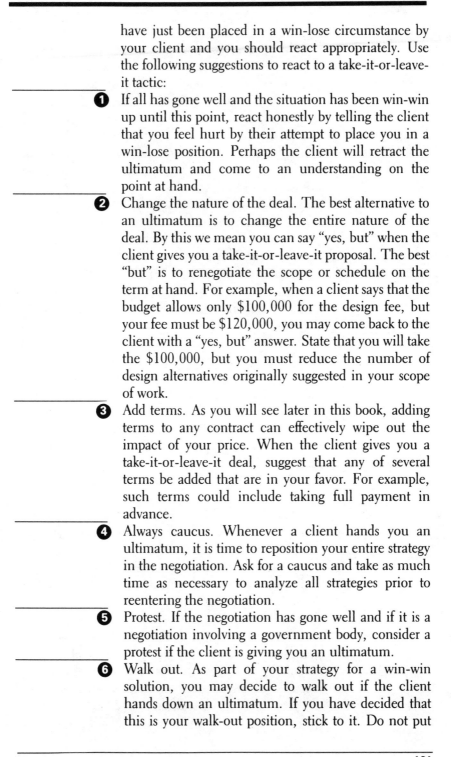

❶ If all has gone well and the situation has been win-win up until this point, react honestly by telling the client that you feel hurt by their attempt to place you in a win-lose position. Perhaps the client will retract the ultimatum and come to an understanding on the point at hand.

❷ Change the nature of the deal. The best alternative to an ultimatum is to change the entire nature of the deal. By this we mean you can say "yes, but" when the client gives you a take-it-or-leave-it proposal. The best "but" is to renegotiate the scope or schedule on the term at hand. For example, when a client says that the budget allows only $100,000 for the design fee, but your fee must be $120,000, you may come back to the client with a "yes, but" answer. State that you will take the $100,000, but you must reduce the number of design alternatives originally suggested in your scope of work.

❸ Add terms. As you will see later in this book, adding terms to any contract can effectively wipe out the impact of your price. When the client gives you a take-it-or-leave-it deal, suggest that any of several terms be added that are in your favor. For example, such terms could include taking full payment in advance.

❹ Always caucus. Whenever a client hands you an ultimatum, it is time to reposition your entire strategy in the negotiation. Ask for a caucus and take as much time as necessary to analyze all strategies prior to reentering the negotiation.

❺ Protest. If the negotiation has gone well and if it is a negotiation involving a government body, consider a protest if the client is giving you an ultimatum.

❻ Walk out. As part of your strategy for a win-win solution, you may decide to walk out if the client hands down an ultimatum. If you have decided that this is your walk-out position, stick to it. Do not put up with an ultimatum. Many design professionals who have accepted ultimatums have gone on only to find out that the client gives ultimatums throughout the course of the contract. This leads to a frustrating and unfortunate relationship throughout the work.

Dealing with "You Have Got to Do Better Than That"

One of the best strategies in any negotiation session is to use the phrase "You have got to do better than that." This puts the other party on the defensive. Whether or not the client thinks you can do better than that, they may design a strategy that uses this sentence at all times. You can use the same sentence in your defense. However, if you are faced with such a circumstance, there are specific strategies to counteract the impact:

❶ Ask what price the client has in mind. Whenever you are told that you must do better than that, respond by asking the client to give you a suggestion as to what they want from you.

❷ Caucus and take a long time to come back. If the client was bluffing by asking for you to do better, he or she will be very concerned about the length of time you are taking to caucus. When you return, open with a question on what price the client has in mind. Again, we reiterate that a caucus gives you an offensive position and puts the client into a defensive position.

❸ Change the scope. As always, a change in scope, if handled properly, can work for you. If the client suggests that you have got to do better than that, consider reducing various aspects of your scope to meet the client's price demands.

❹ Use a value engineering concept that reflects your entire fee as part of the lifetime cost of the project. To do so draw a pie chart, as in Figure 7-1, showing that your fee is less than one-tenth of 1 percent of the entire cost of the project over the duration of the 20-year life cycle of a project. Suggest to the client that by reducing your price any further, he or she will be jeopardizing the biggest and most significant cost of the project, that of operating expense over the life of the project. Develop a whole series of benefits that you

● Figure 7-1. Fees as a Percentage of the Life Cycle Cost of a Project

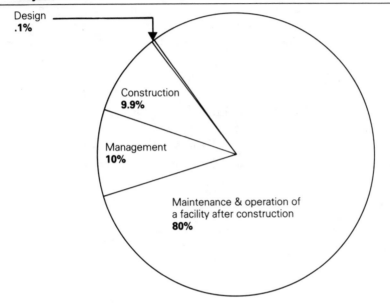

Design
.1%

Construction
9.9%

Management
10%

Maintenance & operation of
a facility after construction
80%

can give to the client and show why you are better than your competition. All this helps to reinforce the point that they should not consider reducing your fee by such a small amount when it could lead to higher costs over the 20-year life of the project.

Demand for the Firm's Top Person

How often have you heard the demand, "We must have the chief executive as our project manager"? Most clients want to deal with the top person in the firm. However, as design professionals we know that it is impossible for the chief executive to be involved in all projects. Whenever a request for specific people is made during the negotiation, suggest that position titles be included in the agreement instead of identifying specific individuals. Doing so allows you to interchange people freely if that is your desire. On the other hand, remember that it may be important for you to identify specific people to attain certain billing rates within your contract. By identifying specific people within the contract, you put yourself in a position to obtain extra compensation if the client later wants to change the personnel.

While the preceding examples of snags in negotiations represent the most common situations faced by today's design professional, there are always circumstances that may come up that are outside your control. Develop a strategy to caucus every time you face an obstacle that seems too tough to consider. Caucusing allows you and your team to sit down and discuss the impact of any client strategy on your entire negotiation. The caucus is a powerful tool and should be used more often in design firm negotiations. Unfortunately, it takes great personal strength to interrupt the negotiation and suggest a caucus. As you enter your next few negotiations, watch how often your clients use this tool to set you off guard. Use it yourself, and plan more effectively how to handle objections raised by your clients.

8 Inking a Deal

- How important is a signed agreement?

- What if you agree verbally but never put it in writing?

- How can you get the client to sign during the negotiation?

- Should you use standard or custom contracts?

- Who should sign an agreement?

- What if your attorney must review everything you sign?

- What is the impact of liability insurance during the negotiation?

One of the most difficult aspects of any negotiation is ending it. Every negotiation session should end with a signed agreement even if it is not totally complete. No one should ever leave a negotiation without getting something in writing, even if it is only handwritten. Leaving the negotiation prior to receiving an agreement only allows the opposing team to further negotiate changes after the session.

In this chapter we explore several techniques for closing the negotiation with a signed contract. Each technique requires practice; you must understand all its implications before putting it to use.

Having the Authority to Sign

In earlier chapters we discussed the factor of authority in negotiations. One of the first tasks that any negotiator has is to determine the authority level of the opposing party. When starting any negotiation, ask if the team members with whom you are negotiating have the authority to sign the contract before you begin your negotiating session. If the opposing party has the authority to sign, you should have already developed a strategy for getting the signature on an agreement prior to leaving the negotiation session.

One of the most common ploys that negotiators use is to stress the importance of having a neat copy of the agreement. If the opposing party volunteers to have the agreement neatly typed prior to signing, reject the idea. Instead, sign even a handwritten agreement that can then be used as the basis for a future typewritten version. Remember that once you have left the negotiation session, your agreement may be reviewed by others within the firm or client body who have the opportunity to suggest modifications to it as written.

Be certain you have the legal authority to sign the contract. In many states, it is required that all partners in an architectural or engineering firm sign an agreement for it to be legal. Check with your state registration board to find out exactly what level of authority is required on a legal contract for design professionals prior to entering a negotiation. Also, be certain to check with your liability insurance carrier to be sure that you have followed all rules required by your carrier so that your liability insurance is not rendered null and void by a premature signing. Remember that if you sign a contract containing anything illegal, your insurance is automatically void. Also, most insurance companies prefer to review contracts before you sign them, which could hinder your ability to sign.

Having the authority to sign the contract correctly and legally is an important step in any negotiation process. Be certain that your authority level corresponds with that needed to sign the document.

When to Sign the Contract Assuming that you have followed the win-win strategy in working toward a mutually beneficial contract with your client, the optimum time to sign the deal is when both parties feel that the scope and terms of the agreement are fully explored and each side has received a fair and just compromise on all items discussed. Never sign the contract the next day or after taking a pause or break for refreshments. Rather, sign an agreement immediately upon conclusion of the negotiation itself. Doing so forces you to be certain that all aspects that you have agreed upon are clearly stated in writing, even if it is just handwriting. It also prolongs the negotiation session itself by forcing each party to scrutinize and discuss what is written. Remember that a longer negotiation provides more chance for a win-win conclusion. By waiting 24 hours or by taking a break before signing, you may be asked to make changes that you are not prepared to negotiate further.

Even if signing means crossing out large sections of a preprinted contract and initialing them, or if it means adding elaborate sections to a preexisting contract, take the time to do so prior to ending the negotiation. There is nothing worse than working long hours on a mutually beneficial agreement only to find that you cannot get a contract signed and that nothing you have agreed upon is enforceable. Remember that your agreement is the only enforceable document to come out of your negotiation session. No matter what your discussions were during the negotiation and no matter how adamantly you attempt to defend your position at every point, unless you have a written document, it is your word against the client's in any court of law.

One design firm in the Midwest uses a building block technique toward achieving written agreement on various aspects of the contract. To do so they immediately write down any incremental agreements reached during the negotiation. Paragraph by paragraph, they build their agreement so that when they are finished with the negotiation, all they must do is rearrange the paragraphs that they have agreed upon to come up with their final written document.

All that this method requires is pencil and paper and the ability to rearrange things into specific sections of a standard contract once the total negotiation process is complete. Using this method, you may often find that many of your signed agreements are nothing more than handwritten pieces of paper. See Appendix B for an example of such a building block contract. Note especially that the building block method is not neat. However, it does cover each and every detail of a contract and is a simple method that any design professional can use.

How to Get Others to Sign

Most architects, engineers, and interior designers want to get a contract signed as fast as possible. However, it is often difficult to get the other party in the negotiation to agree to sign a contract at the end of the negotiation session itself. There are several techniques that can be used to initiate the signing of an agreement or to encourage the opposition to think about ending the session when you have both come to agreement on most issues, terms, and prices.

Bring Preprinted Agreements. Having preprinted agreements such as the standard AIA or NSPE documents allows the design professional to pull out such an agreement toward the end of the negotiation in anticipation of signing. Doing so signals the other party that you are ready to close the negotiation and that you wish to have a signed contract before leaving. It also raises the question of a discussion of the specific terms of billing and payments as part of the negotiation process. We recommend that everyone should have some sort of preprinted or pretyped agreement available to pull from their briefcase toward the end of a negotiation to facilitate signing of the contract.

Taking such a small physical action as pulling a contract from your briefcase is a strong signal to an opposing negotiator. You may find that such a signal prompts the opposing party to resist signing and to prolong the negotiation session itself. If this is the case, you can be certain that all aspects of your agreement have not been ironed out and that you do not have a win-win situation. In a true win-win situation, both parties will be eager to sign an agreement because both feel they have given and received during the negotiating session.

Stand Up and Put Your Coat On. By indicating to the opposing party that you are ready to leave the negotiation session, you are implying that it is time to reach an agreement. Standing up, putting your coat on, or finishing your coffee are all actions that imply departure. Take a physical action such as this and then follow it by displaying a preprinted contract. Only through an active effort to close the negotiation session will many negotiations end.

Another technique is to pull out a pen and ask the other party for a contract to sign. Doing so will determine whether or not your opposing negotiator is prepared with his or her own prewritten agreement. Always have your business or corporate seal with you during the negotiation so that if a legal signature is required, it can be supplied. However, remember that having the seal does not mean that you *must* use it. Not having it means you cannot.

Fulfill All Legal Requirements. Getting others to sign correctly may require that their organization prepare legal meeting minutes for the corporate meeting book. In advance of the negotiation session, research the laws covering both parties to the negotiation to be certain that all necessary "tools" for the signature of a contract are available during the negotiation session. It does no good whatsoever to reach a final agreement only to find out that neither party can legally sign the agreement.

Emphasize Details. When attempting to close a deal, one of the surest methods to help with a closing is to emphasize that only a few minor details remain. Putting the emphasis on details assumes that the big picture is settled and that all the major terms have been readily agreed upon. Now all that remains is to cover a few minor details in the agreement before closing. For example, try to work out the details of reimbursable expense pricing after all aspects of scope have been covered. By dwelling on the details of reimbursables, you are suggesting that all other aspects of the project have been covered.

Suggest Benefits of Signing Now. If you are having difficulty getting the other party to arrive at a closure, emphasize a series of benefits that would be lost if the agreement is not signed now. For instance, your project schedule may not be met unless the agreement can be signed and put into action today. Or Mr. Jones may not be able to act as your project manager if you don't reach a signed agreement today, since there is pressure from other partners in the firm to use Jones on other projects. Or point out that soil borings may not be done before winter if the agreement is not signed by November 1. Each of these examples highlights a benefit that could be lost by your client if the agreement is not signed expeditiously. Brainstorm to come up with a series of benefits that would be lost on any potential project if the agreement is not signed in the negotiation session.

Give Special Inducements to Sign. When planning your negotiation, one technique you can use to get a quick closing is to develop a list of three or four specific inducements for the opposing party to sign the contract when you want them to. This is a more positive approach than pointing out benefits that will be lost or potential threats to the client, and it provides a strong incentive to sign immediately. Some examples of inducements to sign include:

1 If the client signs now, you will assign partner John Smith as the special project manager.

2 If the client signs now, you will charge no mileage for reimbursables, since you have an additional project in that area and will be visiting it anyway.

3 If the client signs now, you will use your brand new computer-aided design and drafting (CADD) system on the project. This will provide a significant benefit to the client that might be unavailable if the client chooses to sign at a later date because of commitments already made for its use by others in your firm.

By developing a list of inducements to sign, you are providing the client with even further reason to use your firm and to sign the agreement when you want them to sign it.

Signing Is as Important as Negotiating

As we said at the beginning of the chapter, one of the most difficult aspects of a negotiation is ending it. Remember that inking the deal can be accomplished if you plan it carefully in advance. To do so, develop a strategy that will allow you to list specific inducements to sign, benefits that will be lost if signing is not accomplished at the end of the negotiation, such as losing the availability of a key person, or physical actions that you can take to inspire the conclusion of the negotiation, such as putting on your coat or taking out a contract. Always have a prewritten contract available, even if it is your own pretyped agreement.

Finally, never leave the negotiation session without a signed agreement, even if it is totally handwritten. Doing so opens up the negotiation process for a complete review and means that many points which you have agreed upon could be changed in a subsequent meeting.

9 Personal Traits of Good Negotiators

- What does it take to be a good negotiator?

- Can you learn specific traits of good negotiators?

- How can you practice becoming better?

- How can you identify positive and negative traits in your opposing negotiating team?

- What gives people power in a negotiation?

- Is it possible to develop personal power in negotiations?

No matter what techniques of negotiating you have learned up to this point, there are still a number of personal traits that any effective negotiator must have. It can be said that some people "have the talent" to be good negotiators while others simply do not. But all the personal traits that we discuss in this chapter can be acquired. However, those individuals who already possess these traits make much more effective negotiators in the long run than those who do not.

In addition, by studying the traits of your opposition, you can determine whether or not they have the capability to out-negotiate you. In this chapter we discuss several tools that can be used to understand the opposition.

Developing Sources of Personal Power

One of the most important traits needed to become a good negotiator is knowing how to develop personal power when little existed before. Doing so requires an understanding of logistics, dress, the role of authority, title, and all other power generators (see discussion in Chapter 3).

Effective negotiators plan their own strategy for developing their power and personal stature prior to walking into the negotiation session. Many will actually rent cars that create the proper image for the negotiation. It can truly be said that your "reputation precedes you" in an effective negotiating environment.

To help you plan to enhance your personal power, use Checklist 9-1. It will aid you in remembering many of the vital areas that should be analyzed prior to entering the negotiation session.

Understanding Traits. In any negotiation it is important to understand the traits of those on your team so that you can use your strengths and weaknesses to the best advantage. Having sensitivity to the assertiveness or responsiveness of those opposite you is also important for analyzing how their actions will determine their negotiating posture.

● Checklist 9-1. Personal Power Analysis

O **Your authority level.** What is it? Is it appropriate for this negotiation? Should it be revealed?

O **Your title.** Is it right for this project? Should it be modified?

O **Enough sleep or rest to negotiate effectively.** Is your flight and hotel planning complete? What if you miss your train?

O **The color of the clothes you're wearing.** Have you studied the impact of color? What does your client expect?

O **How you arrive.** Should you rent a limo? Car? Taxi?

O **How your phone is answered.** Does a private secretary answer for you? How long does it take to get through to you?

O **Signs of power (diamonds, high-priced watches, and so on).** Should you rent some for the negotiation? Is your briefcase new or ragged?

O **Preparation.** Is your planning sufficient? Do you have a contract in your briefcase?

O **Logistics.** Do you know where you will negotiate? Are you prepared to control seating?

O **Reputation.** Has it been established for you? How can you enhance it when you walk in?

O **Others with you in the negotiation.** Should you bring more or less? Is the chief designer appropriate?

O **Opening remarks.** How can you set the stage for success? What should you say first? Who should start?

One excellent method of identifying overall behavioral patterns of various members of any negotiating team is a test devised by Wilson Learning Corporation. It involves the scaled ranking of each individual with respect to their responsiveness and assertiveness. Those who tend to keep to themselves are given a low responsiveness number; the gregarious and group-oriented are given a high responsiveness number. With respect to assertiveness, those individuals who are self-starters are given high numbers; those who tend to seek direction from others are given low numbers. When a grid is prepared with responsiveness on the x-axis and assertiveness on the y-axis, the personality of each team member can be plotted at the

● Figure 9-1. Behavioral Traits of Negotiating Team Members

GUIDELINE FOR RECOGNITION
HOW RESPONSIVE IS THE PERSON? HOW ASSERTIVE IS THE PERSON?

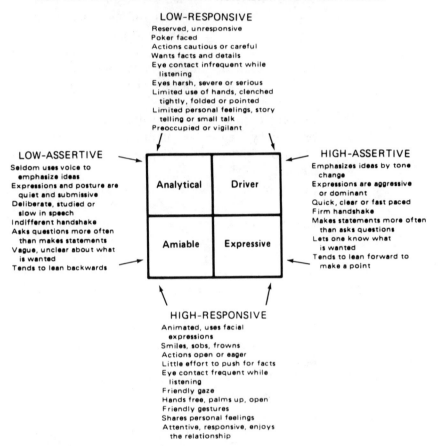

LOW-RESPONSIVE
Reserved, unresponsive
Poker faced
Actions cautious or careful
Wants facts and details
Eye contact infrequent while
  listening
Eyes harsh, severe or serious
Limited use of hands, clenched
  tightly, folded or pointed
Limited personal feelings, story
  telling or small talk
Preoccupied or vigilant

LOW-ASSERTIVE
Seldom uses voice to
  emphasize ideas
Expressions and posture are
  quiet and submissive
Deliberate, studied or
  slow in speech
Indifferent handshake
Asks questions more often
  than makes statements
Vague, unclear about what
  is wanted
Tends to lean backwards

HIGH-ASSERTIVE
Emphasizes ideas by tone
  change
Expressions are aggressive
  or dominant
Quick, clear or fast paced
Firm handshake
Makes statements more often
  than asks questions
Lets one know what
  is wanted
Tends to lean forward to
  make a point

| Analytical | Driver |
| Amiable | Expressive |

HIGH-RESPONSIVE
Animated, uses facial
  expressions
Smiles, sobs, frowns
Actions open or eager
Little effort to push for facts
Eye contact frequent while
  listening
Friendly gaze
Hands free, palms up, open
Friendly gestures
Shares personal feelings
Attentive, responsive, enjoys
  the relationship

Recognition is most accurate by observing one dimension at a time.

intersection between their rank for assertiveness and responsiveness, as shown in the example in Figure 9-1. It is also useful to rank the client, partner-in-charge, third-party agencies, and anyone else heavily involved in the negotiation and plot their points on the same grid. (There are no good or bad positions on the grid; each quadrant simply represents a different type of personality and style of communicating.)

Those in the northeast quadrant are "drivers," or control-takers. They are highly assertive, but not very responsive. In a crisis, they will attempt to resolve the problem by themselves without outside interference.

Persons in the southeast quadrant are "expressives." Their high level of responsiveness and assertiveness makes them flexible in dealing with a variety of situations. They tend to be good with ideas, but often lack the patience to follow through with the details. In a crisis, they attempt to involve a number of people in order to achieve a democratic resolution and may spend too much time arriving at a decision.

Those in the southwest quadrant are "amiables," or support-givers. Amiables mix well in groups and tend to do well in marketing situations where social contacts are important. In a crisis, the amiable tends to blame others.

Individuals in the northwest quadrant are "analytics," or data collectors. They tend to be cautious in making decisions, thorough in dealing with every detail of a problem, and place quality ahead of budgets or schedules. In a crisis, the analytic usually avoids the problem, leaving it for someone else to resolve.

In a typical negotiation, it may be good to have drivers, expressives, amiables, and analytics all represented on the team, so the team leader can make best use of each one's style for various tasks. For example, if you need to negotiate a special contract term with a lifelong bureaucrat, this task can best be handled by an amiable, who can establish rapport with the official. Involving a driver in this activity would probably result in animosity and jeopardize the objective of obtaining the term as part of your agreement.

The negotiator's challenge is to (1) recognize the basic personality types of each person involved in the negotiation, (2) make best use of each individual's behavioral traits, and (3) avoid conflicts by minimizing interaction between people of opposite personality types. As chief negotiator you should also identify your own personality type and review how you interact with others.

Dealing with Negative Thinkers. You often must deal with "negative thinkers" who have been assigned to the negotiating team. These individuals are characterized by the following behavioral traits:

❶ *Egotism.* Negative thinkers tend to be argumentative and will not hesitate to insult anyone who does not agree with their opinions. The objective of this behavior is for the negative thinker to elevate his or her position by lowering that of others.

❷ *Perfectionism.* Negative thinkers view the world in absolute terms. This view requires them to go to extreme lengths to achieve perfection, ignoring the fact that most design decisions are compromises among performance, cost, and schedule.

❸ *Procrastination.* Managing time effectively conflicts with the negative thinker's desire for perfection. Every deadline therefore becomes a last minute panic and most of them tend to be missed.

❹ *Distraction.* Taking off on tangents not only assists negative thinkers in their quest for perfection, it also helps avoid completion of an assignment.

George A. Pogany, a department head at Shell Research Company in Holland, offers the following advice on how negative thinkers operate and how you can harness their competitive spirit and energy.

❶ Don't allow yourself to be drawn into arguments about details. Acknowledge minor problems, but confine the discussion to overall project objectives.

❷ Don't assign negative thinkers to tasks that require simple and quick solutions. They will perform much better where the emphasis is on attention to detail.

❸ Recognize that, handled correctly, negative thinkers can be very useful assets. Their attention to detail may often uncover contract defects that others have over-looked. Also realize, however, that they are a luxury. You cannot afford to have too many of that kind around.

④ Help to change the negative thinker's style by pointing out the results of actions you feel were deliberately destructive.

Specific Traits Found in Good Negotiators

As you read this section of the book, keep in mind the negotiators whom you rate as excellent. Each of these negotiators probably has many of the traits that we will now discuss. Each trait can be learned with proper study. However, having all these traits alone does not assure that you will be effective at negotiating. You must also follow many of the techniques for planning, organizing, and directing a negotiation session outlined in the preceding chapters. Then having these traits will enhance your ability to be an effective negotiator of design firm contracts.

Patience. One of the most important characteristics of a good negotiator is the ability to have patience. Being patient in a negotiation will often leave the other party to commit too much or to "play all their cards" before you have to give up any position. Having patience often means listening to *how* things are said instead of to *what* is actually said. It also means resisting the natural tendency to let your ego get involved in the negotiation session. Remember that you have all the time in the world to conduct your negotiation, and patience can be your strongest trait in any effective design firm negotiation session.

During the Vietnam peace talks in Paris, the Vietnamese representatives displayed an incredible amount of patience. Not only did they move their entire families to Paris and purchase residences prior to the talks, but during the negotiation they also took a great deal of time to analyze each and every aspect of the demands that were being placed on them by the United States. Recognizing that significant pressure was being placed on the American negotiators by citizens at home, the Vietnamese were patient enough to wait for a settlement that was very much in their favor. You too can develop a patient attitude if you plan your strategy that way.

Planning Skills. Every effective negotiator is a planner. Good planners make good negotiators. The ability to plan every speech or every sentence prior to speaking is an important trait of a good negotiator. Thus, the ability to plan is a trait that should be looked for when searching for effective negotiators. Those who cannot plan effectively should not be allowed to conduct a negotiation session. You may find yourself giving away more than necessary simply because adequate plans have not been made.

High Tolerance for Ambiguity. Because many things are being said at once in most negotiation sessions and because very few are nailed down immediately, a good negotiator must be able to tolerate and deal with many ambiguous statements. For example, suppose a client has not yet finalized the program for renovating the interior of a new computer facility. You may be asked to negotiate on a series of "what-if" circumstances, never sure whether the client may change the program after you have even completed your agreement. Thus, anyone who is overly finite in their approach to negotiation may find themselves in trouble with a skilled client.

Ability to Perceive Power. One of the most important traits in a good negotiator is an ability to perceive power. When entering a room, ask yourself if you can perceive which people in the room have more power than others simply by observing the way they are dressed or how they conduct themselves. Also, listen very carefully to those who speak to determine what level of power each has in that particular environment. Every social gathering has a power hierarchy. A negotiation session is no different. Within the session itself there are people who have power based on their authority. However, there are others in the negotiation who have more power simply based on their interpersonal skills.

One design firm in Cambridge, Massachusetts, discovered, much to their chagrin, that personal power can be more important than authoritative power. When negotiating with a major university in New England, the project manager for the design firm addressed most of his comments to the chairman of the board of the selection committee. However, there was a very vociferous woman on the committee whom the design firm had not met prior to this negotiation session. Not having done their homework and not recognizing the power of this individual, the comments by the design firm side were not addressed to her. After the negotiation session, the firm was informed that it had not been awarded the contract. Research into the matter revealed that the woman was an art historian who had convinced members of the community to remove the design firm from the project because of its insensitivity to herself and the historical requirements of the job. Not only had she wielded personal power, but she had gotten others in the community to join her side. This is an example when members of the committee who had more "power by title" deferred to the personal power of an individual on the board.

Thus, the ability to recognize the personal power of those opposite you in the negotiation is a very important trait of a good negotiator.

Verbal Ability. Good negotiators simply cannot speak poorly. A good negotiator must have correct verbal skills so that when ideas must be stated they are clear and concise. Having verbal ability means that the negotiator should not stumble over word usage or use grammar incorrectly. For example, using spoken phrases like "you know" or "yeah" or "um" indicates poor verbal skill. You should also use appropriate eye contact and speaking techniques so that what is said is clearly understood by those who are listening.

Tactfulness. Good negotiators are tactful. Remembering that the strategy in most design firm negotiations is to achieve a win-win solution, it is important that a good negotiator not injure the reputation or insult those with whom he or she is negotiating. Tactfulness is the ability to get your point across without offending the opposing party. Often it is not *what* is said, but *how* it is said that creates a problem. Tactful negotiators know exactly how to word a sentence to achieve the optimum results in a win-win environment. For example, a tactful negotiator would ask the client a question such as "Would you agree that the program would be better with four nursing units instead of three?" instead of saying, "I think the project would be better with four nursing units."

Ability to Think Clearly Under Stress. Good negotiators think clearly in all stressful situations. Of course, the negotiation session itself is a stressful environment. Added to this is the ambiguity created by the uncertainty over terms, and you realize that each negotiator must continually operate in a stressful situation. If stress causes a negotiator to make decisions that are ineffective and that work against the planned strategy for the negotiation, then he or she should be removed from the session. The best way to develop the ability to think clearly under stress is to practice. Therefore, it is important to involve as many people as possible in your firm in mock negotiations so they will gain valuable "stress-thinking" experience. The ability to think clearly under stress is vital for the success of a negotiation.

A Good Sense of Humor. At one negotiation session for a mechanical design subcontract on a project, two design firms were hopelessly deadlocked after six hours. The lead principal for the architectural firm picked up a pitcher of water to pour himself a glass and while talking proceeded to pour the water directly on the table and his notes, totally oblivious to the fact that he even had the pitcher in his hand.

Because he kept pouring the water, everyone in the room broke into an uproar of laughter, and soon the deadlock was broken and the negotiation completed successfully.

Using humor in the appropriate situation can create an effective environment for a win-win condition. Effective negotiators know how to use humor and emotion appropriately.

Analytical Ability. Good negotiators are analytical. They have an ability to perceive numbers clearly, and they can quickly analyze situations to their firm's best interest. An analytical ability means that a negotiator can understand a question posed by the opposition and determine its entire impact on your negotiating position in a brief period of time. Without such analytical ability, a team of negotiators could easily "give away the store" without even realizing it. For example, a negotiating team that is unfamiliar with the effect of an increase or decrease on a firm's fee multiplier on direct labor could get into serious trouble and lose a great deal of money without knowing it.

At one negotiating session in the Northeast, a client asked a team of architects for their multiplier. Without hesitating the lead individual in the negotiation quoted a figure of 2.8. Never did the client ask on what the multiplier was calculated, and so the design firm was able to invoice the client for 2.8 times direct personnel expense (payroll costs), getting an effective direct labor multiplier of 3.65 times direct labor for the firm's contract. In this case the client was the loser, and the design firm was the winner, but in many cases design professionals are not adequately prepared to analyze quickly the impact of such questions on the firm's financial structure. For example, suppose a client asked you to reduce your overhead from 1.51 to 1.39 but to increase your profit by 2 percent and your overall multiplier from 2.89 to 2.93. Would it be a good deal, and could you answer quickly?

Ability to Use Emotion. American negotiators, especially design professionals, tend to be too unemotional in a negotiation. Perhaps it is fear of offending the client that causes design professionals to be so reserved. However, emotion can be a powerful tool in a negotiation. A good negotiator knows how to control emotion to get the best effect in a negotiation session. There is a time to use anger and a time to use patience. There are also times to raise or lower your voice. And there is a time to create an emotional response to a situation. We all remember Nero playing his violin while Rome burned, yet how many of us remember why it was done or what caused Rome to burn? Likewise, emotion can have a significant effect on the outcome of a design firm contract.

Can Be Practical. Good negotiators are practical. It does no good to ask for something that is not achievable. A good negotiator knows the client's limits together with the limits of the firm prior to entering a negotiating session. Practicality means that a good negotiator will not push the client beyond what is reasonable within the client's own organization. Likewise, a good negotiator does not allow a client to push his or her own organization beyond its capabilities. For example, if a client asks your firm to take on a new technical problem, it would perhaps be better for you to suggest hiring another specialist than to accept the client's challenge and take on something beyond the firm's capability.

Has Integrity. The integrity of a negotiator in the design professions is critical. In fact, clients often look for a firm with a reputation for integrity. In most situations the unethical, unscrupulous negotiator is not respected by the opposing negotiating team. Thus, an effective negotiator must maintain high morals and a high level of integrity throughout the process of negotiating.

The Ideal Negotiator

If there was an ideal negotiator in your firm, that negotiator would have several traits crucial to the success of the overall negotiation. He or she would have an ability to negotiate effectively within his or her own organization for salary increases or positional assignments. He or she would be willing and able to plan carefully and to know the services offered. He or she would also have the courage to probe and check vital information necessary to the effective definition of scope and budget on the project. The effective negotiator would have good business judgment and an ability to discern real bottom-line issues for the firm. The ideal negotiator would be able to tolerate conflict and ambiguity well and have courage to commit the firm to higher targets and take the risks that go with it.

The ideal negotiator has the wisdom to be patient and to wait for the opposing party to unfold the story. In addition, there is a willingness to get involved with the opponent and the people within his or her organization to understand the most minute need of the client. The ideal negotiator would also be committed to a high level of integrity and to the conclusion of a win-win solution on the project.

Good negotiators possess the ability to listen carefully with an open mind to all positions offered by the client. They have the insight to view negotiations from both a personal standpoint and an organizational standpoint so that the hidden personal issues that affect the outcome can be clarified and analyzed carefully. They are willing to use team experts as subconsultants or others within the project to get advice on areas with which they are unfamiliar. And finally, they are stable. A person who is confident in his or her own capability, who can negotiate and laugh without too strong a need to be liked, such a person is the ideal negotiator for a design firm contract.

Part 3

Special Concerns

Because every negotiation is different, it is important to explore some of the general areas of special concern related to particular types. In this part such topics as the circumstances unique to government negotiations will be discussed, as well as specific contract clauses to help you limit liability and make more money.

10 Specific Contract Terms

- Is there any way to overcome a wide price differential with specific contract terms?

- What term can you use to ensure that the client will pay?

- How can you keep track of client changes more effectively?

- Is it possible to limit liability using a contract term?

- Can you split the savings with a client on work that costs the client less than expected?

- Are there special reimbursables you can charge as extras?

- Can you be paid entirely in advance?

There is an old saying that in a design firm contract, one term can be worth a million dollars if it is the right term for that contract. In this chapter, we outline several specific contract terms that can effectively minimize your losses on a contract that is undervalued. In addition, use of some of these terms can improve your profitability on the contract. Each term is nontraditional and therefore should be used with the full knowledge of your liability carriers. Remember that no single term alone can completely make up any significant monetary difference. However, should you use all or a number of the terms included in this chapter together, you will undoubtedly improve the financial performance of all projects in which they are used.

Clauses to Add to Your Very Next Contract

Prior to discussing each of the individual terms that we suggest you use, let us presume that you are in the eleventh hour of a negotiation session with a client for a large municipal facility and that the fee for the project offered to you by the client is $100,000. Furthermore, let us assume that having explored all aspects of scope and all the traditional terms, your lowest possible quotation on the project is $120,000. How can you effectively take the project for $100,000 and not lose $20,000?

The following terms offer several suggestions on how to close a gap of plus or minus 20 percent on a project, allowing you to take projects for less than your desired fee and still make money. Keep in mind this example as you explore each of the terms discussed below to discover if they are applicable to your firm.

Let the Client Do Some of the Work. Many design firms today receive much assistance from clients. You can allow your clients to provide you with as-built drawings of existing facilities or to measure site dimensions or the dimensions of a building under renovation. In addition, the client in today's world can provide you with photographs or actual drawings by their own staff. However, few design professionals think of some of the more mundane services that could be provided by a client.

Ask yourself how much you spend annually on your messenger service. In your next contract, suggest that the client come to your office to pick up drawings or messages rather than having your message service deliver them. By asking your client to pick up drawings at your office, you may save $1000 to $2000 in overhead expenses during the course of the project. This will effectively reduce your losses by $1000 or $2000. Likewise, your client could provide its own blueprinting service, eliminating the necessity of your charging them for that reimbursable. Look for simple yet effective ways to have the client do some of the work necessary to the project.

Suggest Special Reimbursables. Should you be forced into a position of losing money on a project, notify the client that they only get coverage of $100,000 or $200,000 worth of project liability insurance on your regular policy. Any additional coverage must be paid for as a reimbursable by the client. Suggesting this alternative to the client could result in a per-project liability policy paid for by the client as a reimbursable expense. If you did this on all projects, it would significantly reduce your overhead by eliminating your professional liability premium.

There are other items that can be treated as special reimbursables. One firm in the Midwest was able to charge rental on a space needed to fit an additional 10 draftspeople who were required for a project. They also rented equipment such as drafting tables, stools, lights, and chairs on a temporary basis and were paid for it by the client. Explore ways to treat normal and traditional items that are part of your everyday scope as reimbursables when you need to do so in an adverse fee situation.

Shorten the Schedule and Work Overtime. There is no doubt that short schedules produce more profitable projects. Discouraging design professionals from being excessively perfectionist and continually redesigning all aspects of the project allows for faster decisions. And faster decisions mean more profitable projects in most cases. Thus, if a client forces you into an inequitable fee situation, suggest to the client that you shorten the schedule and work overtime to accomplish it. If the project is being invoiced on an hourly basis, working overtime can provide the additional bonus of higher salary rates within your multiplier.

Get a Retainer or Full Payment in Advance. Whenever you are forced to take a fee that is not equitable to your firm, get a retainer or full payment in advance. Especially with new clients, you should seek to get a retainer or full payment on all projects. When you receive this retainer, do not apply it on a prorated basis to all invoices throughout the project. Instead hold it in an interest-bearing account until you send the last invoice on the project. The surest way to avoid bad debts is to have cash in the bank whenever you submit your final invoice. It is better if you owe the client than if the client owes you money, which has the potential of becoming a bad debt at the end of the project.

Shorten Your Billing Cycle. Improved cash flow means that you can reduce interest charges in your firm or in fact earn interest on monies received. If a client forces you into a less than equitable fee position, always work toward shortening your billing cycle. One firm in the Northwest, which won a major hazardous waste contract, invoices their client daily, because the fees are so significant that a 24-hour period without cash makes a difference in year-end earnings. What must be balanced out in this process is the cost of typing and managing a large number of invoices versus the cost of allowing the client to hold on to your money. Also remember, shortening the billing schedule makes it easier for the client to pay, since all invoices will be smaller. In addition, you will receive a steady flow of cash instead of waiting for the end of a long phase or the end of a period to bill.

Simplify Your Billing. If a client asks you to reduce your fee by $20,000 and you must do so under duress, insist on conditions. For example, say that your billing format must be simplified. Eliminate tedious justification for every charge on your invoice and simply use one-line invoices adding to the sum that you have agreed upon. Eliminate the necessity for backup copies of justification for every reimbursable on an invoice. Instead provide a term allowing the client to audit all expenses invoiced to them. Be sure to include the invoice format as part of your negotiations. The invoice format can create havoc in an accounting department, especially when more than 90 or 100 projects are all invoiced independently with different formats. Simplify your format and invoicing procedure, and include these as important terms to every negotiation. Figure 10-1 is an example of a simple design firm invoice to suggest to problem clients.

Get Guaranteed Interest. Although most clients resist paying interest, if you are being asked to take a reduced fee, you should insist on being paid properly. Allow the client to set the interest rate for penalties if prompt payment is not received. Doing so encourages the client to pay, since they have had a part in setting the amount of the penalty. Therefore, a discussion of late charges should be included at every negotiation for which you are reducing your fee. It is only fair that you should be paid promptly if you are reducing your fee below what you expect or deserve to receive.

Limit the Liability. When taking a reduced fee, you should always limit your liability to the amount of your net contract for the project. The net contract is the amount of money received by you minus any payments to subcontractors or other design professionals, minus any reimbursable expenses that are pass-

ABC CLIENT

1000 City Street

Anyplace, USA 00000

RE: RENOVATION PROJECT

INVOICE

For professional services rendered per agreement for the period ending 3/31/85 as follows:

Professional Design Fees	$3,000.00	
Plus: Reimbursable Expense	400.00	
Current Total Due	$3,400.00	

Thank you sincerely,

Professional Designs, Inc.

---

throughs on the gross amount. Design Professionals Insurance Corporation (DPIC) even offers a reduced liability insurance premium for those firms that are able to specify a limit of liability term within their contract. If you are able to achieve a limit of liability term on all contracts, you may significantly reduce your overhead by cutting your liability premium.

Keep in mind that you cannot eliminate liability altogether, and you cannot reduce the impact of third-party lawsuits on your firm. (Third-party lawsuits are those in which a completely innocent bystander is affected by the project.) However, you can eliminate the majority of claims between yourself and your client by limiting your liability to the amount of your fee. In addition, whenever a claim is made by your client against you, if you have a limit of liability clause, you are assured that you cannot lose more than what you have already received from the client.

Split the Savings on Underbid Work. A new term that seems to be in more frequent use today in design contracts is a split on savings of underbid work. To achieve results using this term, it is important that independent estimators evaluate the project immediately after the initial design is finalized between you and your client. If a construction estimate can be agreed upon at that point, the objective of this term is to benefit you if the construction bid comes in later under the estimate provided by the independent estimator. The term should be written so that a split of the savings on underbid work is given to you if the job comes in under the bid. However, if the job comes in over the bid, the client should bear 100 percent of the expense for any overbid work.

Although this term may seem unfair to the client and although you may not be able to get it in your contract, keep in mind that you have alrady agreed to a loss ($20,000 in the example given at the beginning of this chapter). By stating your upfront loss to the client, you may be able to include a term providing a split on underbid work without any penalty to you if the construction bid then comes in over the earlier estimate.

Have the Client Sign Drawings. One of the most difficult items to measure during the course of a contract is the amount of change that occurs in drawings. By including a term in your contract that requires the client to sign drawings on five to seven calendar dates spaced evenly throughout the course of the job, you are ensuring that the client is aware of changes made at a specific point in time. If you must then go back to the client to attempt to collect for changes, your documentation is much more specific, and it will be easier to prove that the client was aware of changes made.

Automatic Escalator. The final term that should be put into every design firm contract is an automatic escalator. In today's AIA and NSPE standard contract, there is a provision for renegotiating contracts after a specified date. However, renegotiation implies that the other party will have equal access to the negotiation and that your fees could go up, down, or remain the same, depending on the outcome of the subsequent negotiation. We recommend that an automatic escalator clause replace the standard clause in those agreements. These escalators will automatically increase the amount of your compensation after a specified date.

Many firms today work under the duress of contracts that do not contain automatic escalators. This means that they work at rates on contracts that were negotiated four to ten years ago and get labor rates that are completely outdated. Had an automatic escalator clause been placed in those contracts, the labor rates could have kept pace with today's inflation.

Automatic escalators should be set at a date that is reasonable yet realistic in terms of the current contract. For instance, if the project's duration is expected to be one year, you may set an automatic escalator into the contract at a period of 18 months from the date of signing. Obviously, neither party has control over some factors that may extend the contract. However, most clients will agree that a project escalator that is 50 percent beyond the duration of the project is a reasonable "trigger" time to establish. Escalators should increase fees a minimum of 10 percent and a maximum of 50 percent, depending on the nature of the escalator and the specific terms involved.

Compensation for Changes One of the most difficult aspects of negotiating a contract is establishing terms that allow for the adequate compensation of changes to the scope of the work. Most design firms wait until they are long into the project before keeping track of or charging for changes. This is a bad mistake and often meets with opposition from the clients. Unfortunately, we cannot blame the clients for such a reaction, since no one wishes to be asked for more money years after a change has been authorized and accomplished.

The most effective way to be paid for changes is to negotiate a procedure for change payment in the initial agreement. Many design firms are fearful of mentioning changes because they think that owners do not want any changes. Unfortunately, all projects have changes, and we recommend that you face the issue of changes squarely at the negotiating table. Ask the client if they expect many changes on the project. If the answer is no, you should be prepared to educate the client about the various kinds of changes that could occur and that are outside the control of either you or the client.

Devise a simple form for keeping track of changes from the first day of a project. One firm in the Northeast devised a form, shown in Figure 10-1, and uses it as follows:

❶ At the negotiating table the client is informed that all changes will be kept track of by the design firm.

❷ The client is also informed that there is an allowance within the fee to take care of small changes, so that the client will not be involved for all changes on the project.

❸ The client is informed that after all "complimentary" changes are used up by the client, the project manager will sit down with the client to discuss changes to date and to review the process for charges for subsequent changes.

❹ The invoice in Figure 10-2 is sent to the client starting on the very first day, whether or not a change is charged for. If no charges are to be billed for a change, the form is marked "no charge." Yet the project manager keeps track of the cost of making the change. Before the contingency budget is used, the project manager can review all changes with the client, showing the client exactly what the cost and the contingencies were for changes that have been made on a complimentary basis for the client.

❺ Once the contingency budget has been used, the project manager uses the form (see Figure 10-1) to provide the client with an estimate of charges for an impending change. Note that on the form a signature

● **Figure 10-2. Change of Scope Form (3 Part NCR)**

PROJ. #_____ PROJECT NAME_____ DATE_____

CLIENT NAME_____

ADDRESS_____

TEL. NUMBER (   )_____ CONTACT PERSON_____

DESCRIPTION OF CHANGE

ESTIMATE/PRICE

SCOPE CHANGE ORDER #_____

APPROVALS

INVOICE _____ Y _____ N

_____   _____   _____

PROJECT MANAGER   CLIENT   ACCTG USE ONLY

155

is required by the client to approve charges. If the signature is not received, the change is not made. For special changes that require telephone notice (such as an urgent demand by a building inspector or other regulatory agent), a form is sent subsequent to the change and must be initialed by the client.

Firms using this procedure and any similar forms have found that a significant number of benefits are derived from analyzing and negotiating a change procedure with a client. For instance, clients don't want to use up their "free changes" and are resistant to acknowledging a free change during the initial stage of a project. Instead, they often argue vehemently that a change was actually part of a quote. Having this argument at the time when the change occurs is significantly better than arguing about it three to five years after the change has been made and the client has forgotten about it.

One of the most significant benefits of negotiating a change procedure is that it requires you to teach your staff about the procedure itself. Most changes are not recorded by design firm staff, and as a result, time is spent making changes without compensation. By teaching your staff the procedures described here and by requiring that all staff be fully aware of the scope of work and enforcing its integrity, your firm will take a giant step toward improving profitability and collecting more for changes. Be certain that you negotiate a change order procedure as part of your contract and discuss all its ramifications with your client before signing the final agreement.

Various Contract Types from a Negotiating Perspective

There are a number of contract types available to design professionals today, ranging from lump-sum contracts all the way to cost-plus fixed-fee (CPFF) contracts with "not-to-exceed" clauses attached to them. Prior to discussing the advantages and disadvantages of each contract type, it is important to consider the basis for the contracts.

In today's design world, it is much more effective to negotiate a value-oriented contract than a cost-based contract. Most design firms today are striving to improve productivity through the use of computer-aided design and drafting (CADD) equipment or through the use of management procedures designed to improve staff efficiency. Under cost-based compensation agreements on which you are paid hourly for time expended on a project, improved efficiency is automatically passed along to clients at no charge. Under value-based compensation arrangements on which you are paid a stipulated sum regardless of how much time is expended by you, improved efficiency results in better bottom-line performance by the design firm.

Unfortunately, during the past 25 years, design professionals have taught clients to use cost-based compensation as the predominant method of payment. Under cost-based contracts, the end result for the profession is a dwindling compensation spiral ending in lower profits and lower compensation for all design professionals. It is important, therefore, when negotiating contracts to keep in mind the difference between value-based and cost-based agreements. The following discussion is emphatically geared toward getting value-based agreements whenever possible.

Lump-Sum Agreements. A lump-sum agreement is an agreement that stipulates a specified total compensation based on the results achieved by your firm's design effort instead of time expended by you. Many lump-sum contracts include reimbursables, but others allow for reimbursables to be invoiced outside the general lump sum. Lump-sum agreements are the most value-oriented agreements in existence. They are value-oriented because the method of performing the work is not part of the compensation arrangement. Thus, if it takes five hours to perform the job or 5000 hours, the compensation is equal and depends upon results rather than costs.

We recommend that all design professionals seek lump-sum agreements wherever possible to minimize the conflict associated with defending costs and to maximize your potential for improving efficiency within your organization. The most significant disadvantage to a lump-sum agreement is that it requires a specified scope of work. Many design professionals cannot specify an exact scope. Likewise, many clients cannot specify scope at the beginning of a project. However, we often find that design professionals simply do not want to specify the scope or go through the contract negotiation process at all. Instead they would prefer to operate on an hourly basis and never sign a contract. Such an attitude will lead to continually reducing fees in the profession as a whole.

Percentage of Construction Cost Contracts. Percentage of construction cost contracts are a quickly dying form in today's marketplace. However, percentage of construction cost is a value-oriented contract, since the performance of duties within the contract is not tied to the compensation method. As a result, the compensation can be value oriented (tied to the construction value) while you can use efficiency-saving devices such as CADD systems to minimize your costs.

Under conditions of inflation, design professionals can profitably do projects on the basis of percentage of construction cost contracts. However, when a downward-turning economy forces contractors to outbid one another for the work, many design professionals have lost their shirts on such contracts. Judge percentage of construction cost contracts carefully, and remember that they are tied to an inflation factor that you may not always control.

Unit Pricing Contracts. Unit pricing is growing in popularity throughout the North American continent. Unit prices are prices that are determined by square-foot amounts of building area or by per-drawing amounts for clients. Unit pricing allows you to establish prices based on the number of units going into a project. It is value oriented in that it allows you to establish your price without regard to what your cost is to produce the unit in question. Be especially careful of unit pricing, however, where large numbers of units are involved. Should the client decide halfway through a project to reduce the number of units below a specified number, you should always negotiate a term into your contract providing for a minimum fee. This avoids the potential problem of stretching your investment in a project that is significantly reduced since there are many basic activities that must be accomplished however large the project.

Cost-Plus Fixed-Fee (CPFF) Contracts. A pure cost-plus fixed-fee contract without a not-to-exceed clause attached to it is a halfway approach to value orientation. The establishment of cost-plus fixed-fee contracts came about as a way to establish the value (fee) of a project to a design firm. However, most government agencies have used cost-plus fixed-fee agreements to thoroughly inspect the cost base of a firm prior to establishing a contract. Doing so forces the design firm to expose all its figures to the client prior to reaching an agreement. Thus, when using this type of contract, there is a strong incentive to increase overhead at the time of negotiating a contract so that an increased overhead factor can be carried throughout the term of the contract. Obviously, increased overhead means less profit on a project, and the incentive to the firm is to increase overhead with allowable deductibles that benefit the firm yet keep the profits low.

Obviously, cost-plus fixed-fee contract arrangements are cost oriented and inspire the firm never to improve its efficiency or use new technology to improve the way in which projects are done. In fact, many firms in the Midwest during the past recession elected not to use CADD systems for government work. Instead they hired hourly workers to perform tasks that could have been easily done on a computer.

Multiple of Direct Labor Contracts. Multiple of direct labor contracts have been in use for years. Unfortunately, a multiple of direct labor contract is an entirely cost-based contract. Cost-based contracts using hours as the unit of sale encourage you to do nothing more than sell hours. As professionals our value is many times more than the hours we sell. However, using a multiple of direct labor or a cost-plus contract compensates us only for the hours that we record on contracts. Our recommendation is that you try to avoid multiple of direct labor contracts wherever possible, except in the dire case of a totally undefined scope.

"Not-to-Exceed" Contracts.

The not-to-exceed contract puts the client into a position of "heads I win, tails you lose." Most design firm clients who are sophisticated understand that a not-to-exceed contract is disadvantageous for all parties concerned. When a project manager has a not-to-exceed contract the tendency is to use every single penny of it and not one more. The incentive for the client is to keep the design firm working after the limit is reached, thereby supposedly getting more benefit for the dollars that it will expend.

A not-to-exceed contract, in our opinion, is a lose-lose agreement. Not only does the design professional lose by having an incentive to spend all the client's money, but the client loses because the design firm will undoubtedly go over the limit and be forced to sustain an unprofitable project at risk to the client, the project, and the design firm alike. Thus, this type of contract should simply be avoided if at all possible.

Combinations of Contracts.

One of the most popular combinations of contract forms in use today is to start with an hourly agreement based on billing rates until the scope of the job can be determined. Note that billing rates are hourly amounts of compensation for work and not cost-based multiples of a person's salary. Thus, a project may start at a $100 per hour billing rate until scope is defined. Once the scope is defined, a lump-sum agreement is structured that either credits the earlier amounts or takes into consideration the scope of work from the point at which a contract is drawn until the bid stage of the project. Note that the lump sum covers all aspects of a project that are under the total control of the design professional. Before the bid stage, the project is out of the hands of the design professional for the most part. As a result, the contract format would change back to an hourly amount with an allowance for observing construction.

A combination contract of this type allows for total flexibility to accommodate both the design professional and the client. The design professional and the client benefit in the early stages by working toward a sound definition of scope without the hindrance of a value-oriented contract. However, once the scope is defined, the designer is given an incentive to work harder to achieve a higher level of profit through efficiency on those tasks within his or her control.

Finally, once the project moves into an area that is controlled by the contractor and not the client or the design professional, the compensation method reverts to an hourly amount to reflect accurately whatever level of effort must be sustained by the design professional during that phase of the project.

How to Negotiate for What You Want

If a client insists on getting a cost-plus fixed-fee agreement on the project, you are faced with a dilemma. How can you get him or her to change the contract form to one more favorable to your firm? Doing so requires a significant amount of salesmanship on the benefits of using the form of contract you want. Therefore, you should brainstorm to come up with a series of arguments to show why your chosen contract format is best. Have this list of benefits with you at the negotiating session, and be certain that all parties on your negotiating team are familiar with it.

Also, you should be prepared to provide specific incentives for the client to use your contract type. For instance, if the client wants an hourly contract and you want a lump-sum contract, suggest that you will give a 10 percent less guarantee if the client agrees to a lump-sum contract. If the client wants a fixed price and you can't define the contract terms, suggest a range of contract fees as opposed to a fixed single amount. Using a range of fees allows you to safely accommodate a variety of circumstances that could occur during a project that has an undefined scope.

You should always be prepared to explain the disadvantages of a not-to-exceed contract to any client. Be specific and be honest, because these contracts provide no incentive for you to be efficient. Perhaps if the client is bound contractually to a not-to-exceed contract, you can insert an incentive clause allowing a split of savings on an underused not-to-exceed amount.

Choose the Best Contract Format for You

Whatever contract type you use for your final agreement, it is important to recognize that the contract becomes the record of the entire negotiating process. Choose the contract format best for you and then sell it to the client, with all the advantages and disadvantages laid out specifically for the project at hand. If you are unsuccessful, have in your repertoire a series of terms that are applicable to your specific firm. In this chapter we have reviewed several such terms, but we are certain that you can add even more to your growing list of specific design firm terms that can benefit almost all contracts.

In today's business world, you should always try to negotiate and reach value-oriented contract agreements, since there is increasing pressure toward improvements in productivity and efficiency. The only way to assure bottom-line profit on a continual basis is to structure value-oriented contracts with terms that don't create win-lose or lose-lose situations between you and your clients.

As a final exercise, review your past five contracts to determine if they were value oriented and if the proper application of some of the ideas in this chapter could have made more money for your firm on those contracts. If the answer is yes, take immediate steps to change the procedures within your firm on contract negotiations.

11 Bidding

- What are the four types of bidding?

- What is the fairest type?

- What specific steps can you take to prevent your client from sharing your scope with others?

- How much information should your proposal include under bid circumstances?

- Are there specific differences in bid contracts?

- What types of clients use bidding today?

- If bidding is unethical, how can you do it in a professional manner?

D uring the past ten years more and more clients have used bidding as a selection criterion for design work. Whenever price is the only selection criterion a bid possibility is present. Although many traditional design firms concentrate in negotiations on the issue of pricing, most deal with the definition of scope in depth and allow the design professional flexibility to adjust scope and price according to a mutually beneficial agreement with the client.

With pure bid selections, there is literally no negotiation. The price becomes the only criterion, and the client is unwilling to discuss any aspect of scope or any other term on the project. Such a situation is definitely a win-lose situation in favor of the client and puts the design professional in the most unfavorable negotiating stance. In this chapter we present several techniques on how to respond when a client asks for a bid on design work.

Whenever economic pressure causes traditional design work to slacken, more clients begin to use price as the only criterion for selecting design teams. Teach your staff how to use the following specific tips on bidding whenever they are faced with a bid situation. Remember that the best strategy to use to avoid bidding is to engage in a long-term educational program to convince clients that bidding is not a viable alternative in the design professions. However, if you are forced to bid, the suggestions in this chapter should help you do so.

Why Clients Use Bidding

Today bidding is used predominantly by small municipal clients who are being forced to bid because of public pressure. With the increase in building costs during the past two decades, local communities have been faced with severe economic constraints. Coupling these constraints with recent budget cutbacks on the federal and state level, many communities see bidding as the only way to reduce the cost of design work. Unfortunately because most municipal agencies and selection committees are made up of citizens who do not understand the nature of design work, they do not understand the impact of bidding on a professional's efforts. In addition, public pressure brought to bear by the press has focused on issues such as the "spare parts war" in which federal government clients have been charged outrageous prices for spare parts that are available in local department stores. These types of pressures, although they are not directly related to the design profession, become central issues in political battles between candidates for public office that focus on the issue of bidding.

Today more private sector clients are also using bidding as a selection criterion. Especially in large corporations, the private sector client has become aware that design professionals who offer similar services can be compared on a price basis. Sophisticated clients such as Digital Equipment Corporation in Maynard, Massachusetts, have hired design professionals themselves to prepare elaborate and detailed descriptions of upcoming projects including tabulations of specific scope items, manpower requirements, and schedule criterion. These clients recognize the value of design professionals and are not attempting to use the low bid in all situations. In fact most private sector clients who repeatedly use bidding do not use the low bidder for a wide variety of reasons. Often the low bidder has forgotten a major portion of the scope and will be placed in a disadvantageous position if it were awarded the contract.

During the last part of this century, we expect to see an increase in the use of bidding as a selection criterion. For this reason, it is important that design professionals teach their professional staffs how to bid design work in an equitable and professional manner. There are many types of bid environments in the marketplace, some of which are described below. However, the most important part of teaching design professionals how to bid is to overcome the psychological barriers to bidding. Most design professionals abhor bidding. As a result, they simply do not want to discuss the subject and in fact fight it on a professional and national level. If it is truly the wave of the future, it is important to take the time to study this chapter carefully and then judge how it can be applied to your firm.

<table>
<tr><td>Four Bidding Environments</td><td>There are predominantly four types of bidding environments:</td></tr>
<tr><td>❶</td><td>Pure bidding</td></tr>
<tr><td>❷</td><td>One-envelope bidding systems</td></tr>
<tr><td>❸</td><td>Two-envelope bidding systems</td></tr>
<tr><td>❹</td><td>Negotiated bids</td></tr>
</table>

Each of these types of bids has come about because different agencies of the government, working under different circumstances, have created a need for a new process of bidding design work. Each is described below, and there are many variations on each type in use in the marketplace.

Pure Bidding. Our definition of "pure bidding" is any situation where a price is asked for in an open marketplace. For instance, if a client asks all design professionals to openly quote a price on a project and then publishes all prices to everyone, the criterion for selection becomes price and price only. In a pure bidding environment, everything is open. There are no sealed envelopes and there is no secrecy with regard to any of the bids.

In most pure bid situations the scope is often ill-defined, and there is little information available on which to make decisions with regard to price. In addition, the client will often respond haphazardly to questions from various design professionals. Thus a pure bid situation is often unfair to the various participants. One design firm may respond accurately to the bid because they have more in-depth knowledge of the project type, whereas another design firm may not be able to respond appropriately because the client himself does not know the specifics of the project when asking for the price. Therefore, pure bid situations represent the most difficult form of bidding in the marketplace.

When you encounter a pure bid situation, the steps

included within this chapter will be of vital importance to your firm. Most design professionals believe that pure bidding is unethical. We agree. Not only does pure bidding create unfair competition, but it also opens up a wide variety of liability questions with regard to the performance of the actual design work. In every case you should resist pure bidding as strenuously as possible.

One-Envelope Bidding Systems. In a one-envelope bidding system, you include both your scope of work and your price in one sealed envelope. The one-envelope system has certain advantages over pure bidding in that it is at least a sealed envelope and keeps all aspects of your proposal as secret as possible. Unfortunately in a one-envelope system, price becomes the predominant factor in selection. Therefore your scope should be limited and the details of your proposals should be as simple as possible so price does not overcommit you to any aspect of the program.

The one-envelope system has been in use in many state government agencies for years. Its primary advantage is that it at least seals the bid. Its primary disadvantage is that the project does not stand separately from the price and cannot be evaluated on the basis of the proposal assembled by the design firm. Therefore price becomes the most predominant factor and many times overshadows a creative approach to doing a project that could result in more effective cost savings during construction.

Two-Envelope Bidding System. Probably the most fair type of bidding in the marketplace is a two-envelope bid situation. Currently in use in many states, the two-envelope bid system allows design professionals to submit a detailed scope of work and proposal in one envelope, with price in another sealed envelope. The client, after judging all proposals on the basis of merit for scope and design criteria, then selects a list of three to five final candidates to do the project. All other sealed price bids are then returned to the respective design firms without being opened.

The price quotes of the final three to five are opened, and the lowest-priced design firm is then selected to do the project.

If you have clients who are being forced to bid because of public pressure or pressure caused by the internal dynamics of the firm, the two-envelope system would be the best one to recommend. It is more fair than the others, mostly because it concentrates on the issue of scope prior to reviewing the prices that have been submitted. Its primary advantage is that it allows for a complete and in-depth review of scope and design criteria prior to an examination of the price. Its primary disadvantage is that it is cumbersome to many clients. However, some clients do not see the advantage of separating price from scope and do not want to invest the time needed to review a wide range of scope proposals prior to examining the price.

Another advantage of the two-envelope system is that it eliminates a small design firm that is "operating out of a garage" from taking a job away from a more qualified design firm. Unfortunately, in a bid situation in which the low price governs, many clients have been severely burned by smaller design firms who have taken on projects that they are unqualified for. Because the two-envelope system requires an in-depth proposal that describes exactly what the design firm will do on the project, it eliminates a small design firm being selected on price and price alone.

Negotiated Bids. In a negotiated bid the firm with the lowest price is chosen, and then a client team negotiates with the design firm to finalize the scope, schedule, team, and all the other details of the project. A negotiated bid is not unlike all negotiated contracts except that the final selection process is based on the lowest price.

Teaching Your Staff How to Bid

Because most design professionals are unaccustomed to bidding for design work, it is important that you take on the task of teaching everyone in your firm how to operate under bid conditions. Whether or not you agree ethically with the concept of bidding, you must recognize that it exists in the marketplace and that sooner or later you will be forced to submit a bid on a project even though you disagree with the concept. Our purpose in formulating these procedures is not to encourage bidding, but instead to help design professionals understand how to achieve the best results in a bid situation.

Whenever you face a client who has no scope definition, there are two prevalent dangers. First, if you overscope the job you may overquote your bid, thereby eliminating yourself from the race. Second (and worse), the unscrupulous client may use your well-defined scope to get prices from other firms.

Use the following steps to teach your staff how to bid successfully.

Bid Only on What You See. The biggest problem with bidding is that most clients so loosely define the scope of work that the exact price figures are nearly impossible to determine. Resist your hereditary professional instinct to further define scope with clients who elect to use bidding procedures. Instead, give exact prices on only what is asked for in the request. Be certain to clarify in your proposal that your price fully covers those items requested and that all other services will require extra cost. Never put in a price for something not requested that you know will be required, especially if the client does not ask for it. For instance, if you know that a zoning variance is required, but the client does not request it, do *not* put in a price for it. You can bill it as an extra service after you get the job, but you may not get the chance if your competitor beats you on price and gets the contract.

Assign a Specific Team to the Project. When making a price proposal, assign team members by name, and do not switch personnel without billing extra charges. Although you will probably be tempted to arrive at your final price by assigning individuals using averaged billing rates, don't! Instead, assign a specific team, and in your contract when you get the job, specify that any deviation from the team members caused by client demands will result in extra charges.

Underscope the Job. Always underscope the job and specify to the client exactly what your price covers. This is necessary because the *low* price gets the job. If your price is higher for *any* reason, you may not get the opportunity to discuss an increased scope.

Copyright Your Scope. Spend the $10 necessary to copyright your scope with the copyright office in Washington, D.C., and inform the client that you have done so. After all, by scoping a project for a client, you are investing valuable time and knowledge. Once you copyright, don't give it away without a fight, and don't decide not to fight if the client doesn't respect it. You may not get the job, but you could teach a client how to operate more professionally.

Specify the Type of Billing Procedures You Will Use. For bid projects, your billing procedures should be twice as tight as normal. Insist on a 20 to 25 percent initial payment held as a retainer. Then identify the exact billing and payment dates in your final contract. Make it clear to the client that all work will stop on the project immediately if you are not paid on the specific payment dates. Also, place into your contract a clause that compensates you for restarting once there is a stoppage caused by any client action. Do not feel sorry for clients who are using bid procedures. Instead, insist on a totally businesslike invoice/payment policy. Charging interest on late payments while continuing work is just not good enough. Stop work and put in penalty clauses.

Insist on a Limit of Liability Clause. Since the client is placing your firm in a precarious position due to their use of price competition, quote bid prices only with the understanding that liability is limited to a specific amount. Then if the client wants a greater amount of coverage, charge for it as a reimbursable. By working in this manner you may also qualify for a reduced fee on your professional liability premium. In today's marketplace, several insurance companies are quoting reduced premiums for liability insurance on the basis of limited liability between the client and the design firm. For instance, Design Professionals Insurance Corporation (DPIC) of California allows up to a 5 percent reduction in premiums on the basis of using specific language to limit liability in your contract.

Expand Your Reimbursables. Instead of sticking with the standard group of reimbursable expenses, expand your list to include such items as:

1. Liability insurance
2. Computer usage
3. Secretarial service
4. Specification service
5. Photography
6. Site inspection
7. Meetings

Although many of these items may normally be included in your work, specify them as reimbursables outside the scope of work included in your fee. Also, set the price of reimbursables (at market prices) per unit instead of basing your price on cost plus 10 percent. Doing so allows you to account for and charge each reimbursable more easily at higher prices.

Insist on a Lump-Sum Contract. The only way to win at bidding is to contract for services on a lump-sum basis. Doing so allows you the incentive to find creative ways to do the work for less. If clients insist on other forms of contract, provide incentives for them to contract on a lump-sum basis. For instance, you may quote a price on a lump sum that is 10 percent below your price for doing it in any other contract format. Of course, having a lump sum means that your bid must be accurately figured and the job must be well managed. On all bid contract types, even percentage of construction cost, be as clear as possible to define exactly what is covered in your price.

Drill Your Team. Before putting in your bid price, assemble your project team and completely review all aspects of the project scope and price. Be certain that everyone who will work on the job understands the nature of your proposal and is prepared to identify extra services before doing them so that appropriate billing can be done. Also review any nonroutine procedures with regard to reimbursables. As the job proceeds, a regular series of meetings on this topic will serve to keep the job in line with your bid price.

Liability versus Bidding. One of the most difficult areas to quantify with regard to a bid for design work is the liability impact of such an activity. Anyone in the business of issuing liability insurance will tell you that bidding as a design firm selection criteria is negative. This is because most insurers can show statistically that projects obtained through bidding have a higher incidence of liability claims. Therefore, whenever you are in a bid situation, you should always consult your liability insurance carrier to be certain that your activities are not jeopardizing your liability coverage. All liability insurance carriers are aware that bidding exists in the marketplace and that you may be forced to participate in this selection process in your practice. However, many of them have active programs of client education, forms, and procedures that can assist you when bidding on a new project. (See Chapter 13 for more thorough discussion of this topic.)

Professionality of Bidding

Obviously, instructions on bidding are going to arouse those of you who most adamantly oppose bidding. However, consider that today your competition may be getting a job, which your firm needs desperately, because it knows how to bid and still win. Price competition does have some worthwhile benefits for our profession that few consider:

❶ Bidding will force firms to manage projects better to survive.

❷ Bidding will hasten lump-sum contracts, thereby placing price on value instead of on cost.

❸ Bidding will force design professionals to be accountable for everything they do—including design.

④ Bidding will improve the financial accounting procedures in most design firms.

⑤ Bidding will drive poorly managed firms out of business, leaving more work for well-managed firms.

⑥ Bidding will allow the best of firms to charge even more as it forces them to spend more on marketing in order to position themselves correctly in the marketplace and to avoid the necessity of bidding. By studying market positioning a firm learns the impact of pricing on position and can structure its marketing efforts to avoid a client who uses bidding as a selection criteria.

⑦ Bidding will make the entire profession more businesslike.

In all other sectors of our economy, price is an issue, and many businesses and professionals are earning far more than design professionals operating in such an environment. You can choose to ignore bidding and risk the consequences, or you can learn how to bid to ensure your firm's future.

The quality of your work is not an issue when bidding, so do not allow yourself to enter the bidding environment unless you are tough enough to adhere to the steps suggested above. But don't ignore bidding either, as more and more clients begin to use it to try to control our already beseiged profession.

12 Foreign Negotiations

- Is foreign negotiating significantly different?

- What cultural differences can you expect in foreign countries?

- How much planning is needed for negotiating a foreign contract?

- How can you research foreign clients?

- Who can you talk to about a specific country?

- Can any U.S. agency help you with foreign negotiations?

- How much do foreign negotiations cost?

U nlike American negotiations, foreign negotiations are radically different, with many of the rules and regulations set out in this book almost useless to you in a foreign setting.

The first word of warning is to anticipate that every foreign negotiation will be completely different. Each country and each hierarchy within the country has its own rules and regulations for conducting its own particular negotiation. In addition, be prepared that foreign negotiations will take significantly more time than their counterpart in the United States. Design professionals have lost often in a foreign setting because they simply do not have the time or resources to sustain a long, drawn-out negotiation. Therefore, read this chapter as a warning to prepare even more diligently for foreign negotiations than you would for stateside ones on a similar project.

How Foreign Negotiations Differ

The biggest difference in foreign negotiations for design contracts stems from basic differences between the American culture and the culture of the country in which you are negotiating. In most countries there is a strong reverence for the authoritative hierarchy. Title and position are earned over generations of family stature, and lower echelon negotiators are bound not to disagree with higher level individuals. Numerous problems can arise, many related to this hierarchical situation, such as:

❶ Repeated negotiations. The necessity of continually repeating negotiations through multiple layers of hierarchical powers until you finally reach the individual who has authority to sign your contract.

❷ Becoming impatient. The tendency to become impatient when you discover that all you have just negotiated is for naught because a higher level authority must approve the negotiation.

❸ Cost. The cost associated with multiple trips to negotiate a single design contract. Because the cost of travel to foreign countries is ever increasing, many design firms simply cannot afford the cost of negotiating an agreement in a foreign country.

④ The language difficulty. Aside from all other difficulties, the innuendoes and subtleties of a foreign language many times can work against you in a contract negotiation.

⑤ The logistics. Because most foreign negotiations occur at the client's site, American negotiators will have difficulty preparing for or controlling the logistical circumstances in which they find themselves.

⑥ Lack of data. Because you are many miles from your home office, it may be difficult to obtain needed project data for continuing the negotiation without having to request elaborate airmail shipping at best or at worst making a trip all the way home.

These are only a few of the difficulties that occur when attempting to negotiate in a foreign country. In addition, because of the monetary differences when exchanging U.S. for foreign funds, the complexities of foreign negotiations often outweigh the benefits. Be certain when you decide to take on a foreign project that you are prepared to negotiate with the full knowledge of all the problems you may incur and with the understanding that foreign negotiations are significantly different than their stateside counterparts.

Traits of Foreign Negotiators

To help you begin to analyze foreign negotiations, make note of the following traits often found among foreign negotiators. Although these traits are common to many American negotiators, they are especially prevalent in the foreign negotiating environment.

Leaving Room to Negotiate. Foreign negotiators must always leave room to negotiate. Whenever you are dealing with a foreign negotiator who is low on the hierarchical scale, that individual must come back to his or her boss with a win. To do so the person must initiate the negotiation by asking for what may seem nearly impossible. Understand that the negotiator does not intend to completely dominate you in the negotiation. In fact, he or she may give up much in the negotiation. However, you must take the position that you should make the individual look good in the negotiation to his or her superiors. To do so you must be willing to give up something and start your own negotiation with room to negotiate. Never quote your rock-bottom price going in or you may end up losing your shirt coming out. The foreign negotiator must feel that he or she has won in the negotiation in order to achieve a mutually satisfying agreement. This is especially true in Middle Eastern countries where family structure is based on those at the top and where those below must prove their worth by winning from foreigners in order to advance in the eyes of the wealthy and powerful sheiks.

Patience. Foreign negotiators have incredible amounts of patience. In one negotiation session for a major hospital project in South Korea, a Massachusetts design firm found themselves enjoying luscious Oriental food combined with elaborate tours of the local historical sites for a seven-day period prior to the one day of negotiations on the last day of the session. It is customary especially in Asian cultures to treat American negotiators as respectfully as possible by showing them the highest level of cultural respect. Be prepared for long, drawn-out negotiations surrounded by festive dining and elaborate entertainment. However, do not be fooled, because the true spirit of foreign negotiators is to ask for an agreement prior to your departure. Foreign negotiators have incredible amounts of patience because they have learned how to negotiate over centuries of hierarchical power.

Effective Use of Emotion. Foreign negotiators are artists at the use of emotion. One design professional reported that during a negotiation for a shopping center in Saudi Arabia, the sheik suddenly stood up, drew out a four-foot sword, and mentioned to the design professional that it was unnecessary to sign a contract. He looked at the rendering of the new shopping center and asked the design professional if the rendering and the final project would look alike. When the design professional answered positively, the sheik turned to him and asked, "You understand what will happen if it does not?," at which time he cut the contract in half with his sword.

Although this dramatic story seems far-fetched, there are many cases in which design firms have entered into agreements in foreign countries without contracts on the basis of effective use of emotion by a foreign negotiator. Therefore prepare yourself for a different type of negotiation by understanding that in foreign countries emotion is often used effectively. Understand that most foreigners perceive Americans as level-headed, unemotional business people and that their use of emotion is calculated to inspire agreement from you.

Trust. In many foreign cultures, it is not necessary to sign written agreements because of a "trusting" relationship that supposedly exists on the basis of a handshake. Do not be fooled by such talk. It is absolutely necessary to secure a written agreement wherever you negotiate a design contract. Prior to entering into the negotiation, you should study enough of the country's culture to understand its traditional customs with regard to agreements. Allowing yourself to be talked into a handshake agreement could be a disaster for you and the firm.

Making Slow Concessions. All foreign negotiators share this trait. They have been taught from birth to concede slowly and always get something for whatever they give. Understand that this trait may make the negotiation appear to be a trading match. However, to most foreign negotiators, the basics of negotiation have to do with trading for value.

How to Protect Yourself

Even though there are many problems with negotiating in a foreign country, it is often lucrative to take on a foreign project. The optimum course of action is to go with an American client into a foreign country. By doing so you will negotiate with an American company on American design concepts even though you will be working in a foreign country. However, should you encounter a foreign negotiating situation, do not enter into the negotiation without adequately preparing yourself for it. Follow some of the rules discussed in this section of the book to protect yourself from foreign negotiators whose goal is to achieve a win-lose situation.

Understand Money. Before entering into any negotiation in a foreign country, study carefully how the U.S. money exchange works with that country. Through resources such as *The Wall Street Journal*, you can clearly learn what the current rate of fluctuation in the money exchange is. However, do not be fooled by a current rate. It is important to know the last 12 months' trend in the money exchange.

You should also completely understand foreign debt implications. For instance, if you want to deal with Argentina today, you might be tempted to negotiate more sternly based on the fact that the government of Argentina could fall because of its international debt. Such a crisis could wipe out a design project and your firm with it. Therefore, it is important that you understand the complete financial workings of the country in which you will negotiate as well as the financial condition of the client.

Ask for Money in Advance. It is customary in foreign countries for clients to pay for services in advance when dealing with a multinational design team. In Australia, for instance, we have conducted many programs and have been paid expenses plus a portion of the fee in advance without question. If the client refuses to pay in advance, it is a sure sign that you may have difficulty collecting later in the project. At worst, you should have client fees placed in a multinational escrow account to be certain that the client can back up any invoices you submit.

Hire Foreign Interpreters. If the contract warrants it, hire yourself a foreign interpreter who understands all the idioms and innuendoes in the country's language. The price you pay for such a temporary consultant will be far less than the price you could pay if a language barrier were to negatively affect your negotiation. Also, when you hire such a consultant, spend enough time with him or her so the person fully understands how you do business. Instruct the interpreter as if he or she were a new project manager in your firm, so that the individual will be completely familiar with your contracts and your operational procedures when entering the negotiation.

Plan Even More. Since you will be negotiating in a foreign environment and since many of the rules of that environment will differ from American rules, you should invest more time than usual in planning your negotiating strategy. It would not be inappropriate for you to visit the client to discuss where the negotiation will be held and what grounds will be covered. In addition, a considerable amount of time should be invested in practice sessions, allowing each of your negotiators the opportunity to review all aspects of the negotiation.

Make airline and hotel reservations well in advance and always fly first class to foreign destinations. Flying coach could leave you stranded in a foreign airport with your client impatiently waiting for your arrival, since coach passengers are not treated as well in many foreign countries as in the United States. To assure yourself an on-time and restful arrival, first class airline travel is the only way to fly when negotiating a foreign contract in a foreign country.

Study also the culture of the country you will visit, and try to find an American design firm that has experience there. Such a firm can point out specific differences or customs to avoid. Get as much project data as possible in advance, and visit a construction company in the foreign location. Also visit a similar project in the foreign country. Remember that each piece of additional data could be just what you need to assure a win-win outcome.

Schedule Double Time. If you expect to spend one week negotiating an agreement for a design project in a foreign country, always plan to spend at least an additional week in the country. By planning for double time in the foreign country, you allow yourself the option of staying for an extended period of time at the request of the client. Never inform the client that you are planning such a schedule, but always be prepared to stay at least twice as long as you expect should the negotiation process require it. Informing the client about your exact departure time "shows your cards." Savvy foreigners will often not begin to negotiate until they know that you are restricted by time pressures.

Prepare for Jetlag. Prepare yourself adequately for the effects of jetlag on your negotiation. Always allow yourself sufficient time to rest and recover from the strain and stress of a long flight. Never expect to negotiate on the day you arrive in a foreign country. Instead, take time to become accustomed to the foreign culture by walking in the city or by touring the sights.

If you are forced to negotiate on a rapid schedule and would like help in dealing with round-the-clock situations, there is an excellent source of such help. Martin C. Moore-Ede, Ph.D. of Moore-Ede Associates, Inc. [Human Performance in Round the Clock Operations, P.O. Box 150, Wellesley Hills, MA 02181 and (617) 235-7964] is conducting extensive research for the National Aeronautics and Space Administration (NASA) on the effects of round-the-clock travel. In his research at Harvard University, Dr. Moore-Ede is studying the impact of sleeping patterns on performance. With the help of such a professional, your negotiating team could be made more effective at a foreign negotiation that requires them to spend an inordinate amount of time in air travel.

Sources of Help

During the past few years, there has been much interest in exporting design services to foreign countries. Moreover, because of huge trade deficits the

U.S. Department of Commerce has developed programs to assist small businesses in exporting their services to foreign nations. In addition, several associations have become involved in specific programs to assist small business people in exporting their expertise. For instance, the Small Business Association of New England (SBANE) at 69 Hickory Drive, Waltham, MA 02154 and at (617) 690-9070 has developed a series of seminar programs and booklets to assist the small business in exporting its services. For further information on other association programs currently available, contact the U.S. Department of Commerce in Washington, D.C., or your local congressperson.

There is no doubt that whatever country you enter you should visit the consulate in your community prior to going abroad for a negotiation. Local consulates can help you verify financial stability of clients in their country as well as gain an understanding of monetary transactions, exchange rates, and customs.

A final source of help is the U.S. Custom Service in Washington, D.C., which can tell you all the customs regulations for foreign entry. Because many countries assess duty on drawings and other materials carried across their border, customs regulations could be a significant part of your negotiation.

| **Be Prepared** | In summary, it is important that you prepare yourself for a variety of unusual circumstances when entering into a foreign negotiation. Review Checklist 12-1 and be sure you can answer every point well in advance of the negotiation. Do not assume that foreigners negotiate the same way Americans do. Do not assume that customs or regulations are similar in foreign countries. Do not assume that you will get help from the United States government whenever a foreign client refuses to pay. Do not assume that a foreign government will help you if a client within its borders refuses to pay you. In fact, do not assume anything. |

Instead, prepare yourself by studying every aspect of the client and country in which you will negotiate.

Expect that your costs will be triple or quadruple what a similar negotiation would cost you in the United States. Plan for recovering the costs of your negotiations in the fee that you quote your client. Otherwise, you will find it too expensive to operate in foreign circles.

Do not run away from foreign negotiations, but do not treat them lightly. Prepare. Prepare. Prepare.

● **Checklist 12-1. Preparing for Foreign Negotiations**

○ Have you investigated specific cultural differences?

○ Do you know how exchange rates are calculated?

○ Have you studied the contract terms carefully?

○ What if you don't get paid?

○ Are there legal remedies available to U.S. firms?

○ Where will you negotiate?

○ Must you use specific foreign subconsultants?

○ What schedule is being proposed?

○ Can you identify an American design firm that has previous experience in this country?

○ What impact does this job have on other work in your office?

○ Can you be paid in advance?

○ Have you calculated the cost of negotiating a contract?

---

13 Liability versus Negotiating Tactics

- What impact does professional liability have on your negotiating strategy?

- What problems cause concern over liability when negotiating?

- Can you limit your liability legally as part of your negotiation?

- How can you be certain that the client understands what you do?

- Are there techniques to improve your listening and communications skills so you do not risk increased liability because of misunderstandings?

- Who can you talk to about liability problems?

A ny book on negotiating would be incomplete if it did not address the subject of liability with regard to negotiating tactics used by design professionals. In every design contract negotiation, you should consult your liability insurance carrier to be certain that you have addressed liability concerns in your tactics for the negotiation.

Prior to signing any agreement, be certain to review it from a liability perspective. Do not hesitate to suggest to your client that the agreement is subject to review by your liability insurance carrier prior to signing. In fact, you might also suggest that insurance representatives from both sides participate in the final contract negotiation session to assure that insurance issues have been covered for both you and your client.

In this chapter we will discuss some of the problems that cause liability exposure such as ineffective communications on project terminology and the impact of overly complex negotiations.

Limited Liability

Today many liability insurance carriers are suggesting the use of terminology to limit a design professional's liability in a design contract. For instance, Design Professionals Insurance Corporation in San Francisco suggests that you and your client limit your liability to the amount of your fee only. An excellent source of information on limiting liability is "Limitation of Liability," a handbook written for members of the Association of Soil and Foundation Engineers (ASFE) [published by the Association of Soil and Foundation Engineers, 8811 Colesville Rd., Suite 225, Silver Spring, MD 20910 and available at (301) 565-2733]. Figure 13-1 is a sample model short form contract from the ASFE handbook, and Figure 13-2 is a model letter to a contractor from the same book. This handbook also contains many sample clauses and other information useful for design professionals. It is a must for anyone who wishes to raise the issue of limitation of liability with a client.

By limiting the liability between you and your client, you may receive favorable treatment by your

Re: *(Name of Project)*

Dear

We are pleased to submit this proposal for services for the referenced project. It is our understanding that the project site comprises some *(area)*, located at and that it is your *(or the owner's)* intent to construct a   thereon.

SCOPE OF SERVICES

Pending further discussion, the scope of our work will include the following services:

(Itemize specific services clearly and concisely.)

Additional services are available from the firm and you may wish to avail yourselves of them. These include:

(Itemize specific services clearly and concisely as a list or as part of a run-on sentence.)

We will be pleased to provide additional information about any and all services provided by this firm and their appropriateness for this project. It is understood that this firm shall be held harmless by you for any and all claims that may arise for its failure to provide services which you specifically direct it to not provide, and that you will indemnify the firm for any costs associated with defense of such claims, and any settlements or awards arising therefrom.

FEES

(If you employ a fee schedule, include the following.)

We propose that our fees be computed on a time and expense basis, in accord with our schedule of charges, a copy of which is attached to this proposal. Given our assumptions relative to the services you will want us to perform, the following identifies the personnel who will be assigned, the estimated time expenditures of each, and the resulting fees:

Personnel (By title)	Hours Required	$/Hour	Total
		TOTAL	$

Please note that this is an estimate based on assumptions and subject to refinement based on further discussion.

(If you do not employ a fee schedule, consider the following.)

Fees for the services we propose to provide for this project will be charged at the rate of *(multiplier)* X the hourly rate of the personnel assigned to the project X the hours worked by each. Once we meet to define the scope of work we will be able to provide a more specific estimate of our fees as well as a "fee not to exceed" maximum. Based on our general understanding of the project, and the services outlined above, we estimate at this time that our fees will be on the order of $ We will invoice you monthly for the work performed and expenses incurred during the preceding month. Payment of each invoice will be due

TERMS AND CONDITIONS

(If you use standard conditions, you can append these to your proposal and establish them as binding for this project through reference here. Otherwise, your conditions should be included here. In either case, ASFE's model limitation of liability clause or one of your own should be included. Legal counsel may advise you to use a typeface which differentiates this clause from other elements of standard conditions.)

We look forward to meeting with you to finalize this agreement and to working with you on this project.

Respectfully submitted,

Encl.: "What Owners Should Know about Limitation of Liability"
"RISK"

Re: *(Name of Project)*

Dear :

         has advised us that you have raised a question about the limitation of liability clause included in the general conditions of the referenced project.

First, let me assure you that limitation of liability is not something new; you are not being asked to participate in an experiment.

Limitation of liability as a general concept is something you probably are already familiar with. You come across it when you travel by air, stay in a hotel, or even leave your car in a parking lot. The pamphlet enclosed gives you more background information. It explains that limitation of liability was first recognized by law in 1601. It has been used by design professionals since 1972.

Limitation of liability's primary purpose is to eliminate a serious problem that has been plaguing the construction industry in recent years. Unscrupulous or incompetent contractors will obtain a project by bidding at or below their cost and, later, in an attempt to gain a profit, will file grossly inflated claims for damages that, they allege, have been caused by deficiencies in contract documents. Because the nature of geotechnical engineering involves so many uncertainties, a disproportionate number of these claims has been directed toward firms such as ours. Despite their lack of merit, all these claims must be defended, usually at considerable expense, thus threatening the very existence of our profession.

Limitation of liability is not at all a "bail out," nor does it ask you to assume our risks or liabilities, or to indemnify us. It does ask you to limit the amount of your claims. Also, as the general conditions make clear, you are asked to review contract documents closely to satisfy yourself that they contain no errors or omissions, and to obtain guidance to clear up any ambiguities. Naturally, this review on your part is in addition to the review we perform. Accordingly, it is very unlikely that there will be errors or omissions. Nonetheless, we are all human and some problems may occur. Because there is a limitation of liability, however, it is to be expected that any and all problems will be called to the attention of responsible parties immediately after they are encountered, so they can be resolved promptly, before they have the chance of growing to major proportions. As a result, the liability we assume on this project—$50,000 *(or, when the fee exceeds $50,000,* approximately $ *)*—should be fully adequate.

Limitation of liability has been applied now to projects whose replacement value is well up in the billions. In no instance have we heard a report of a contractor feeling that the limitation imposed an unfair burden. In fact, many contractors are much happier working with limitation of liability, because it eliminates from competition the "low ballers" who gain a "competitive edge" through unethical and dishonest dealings.

I hope that this letter and the enclosures are sufficient to address your concerns. If not, please give me a call. I will be happy to discuss this subject with you at greater length.

Sincerely,

Encl.: "What Contractors Should Know about Limitation of Liability"
     "RISK"

insurance carrier when premium time arrives. The Design Professionals Insurance Corporation reduces its premiums if you are able to negotiate a contract with a limit of liability clause in it. For specific contract language, you should contact your liability carrier and determine the firm's rules and regulations with regard to limit of liability.

Warning. Note that liability limitations cannot be applied to third-party lawsuits. Whenever an innocent bystander falls on your construction site and an injury results, he or she will sue everyone in sight. Third-party lawsuits are the predominant cause of high liability premiums due to overzealous prosecution in the courts. However, limitation of liability between you and your client will go a long way to reducing your liability premiums and to helping your negotiation be more of a win-win for both you and your client. Appendix C is a list of clauses prepared by Atlanta attorney and noted architectural/engineering consultant Paul M. Lurie, Esq., that can be used to limit liability. Be certain to check with your own advisor before using this material.

Communication

One of the biggest problems discussed by many insurance carriers is the poor communications that take place between clients and design professionals. Often this poor communication results in liability claims that could have been avoided had proper communication identified problems before they occurred. This happens most often when a client assumes that a specific service is normally part of the design service, but you do not include it in your discussions during negotiating. Measuring existing dimensions, obtaining permits, and providing unlimited sets of prints are examples. Therefore, negotiating is a communication process, which encourages you to talk directly with your client about each specific contract term.

Listening. Take advantage of the process by listening carefully and by discussing clearly all aspects of the project at hand. To improve your listening skill, ask yourself the following eight questions prior to entering the negotiation:

1. Make a list of points of acceptable listening conduct. Is it all right to read a paper, write a letter, and so on?
2. What are your particular strengths or weaknesses as a listener? How do you listen?
3. What factors tend to distract you and take your mind off the speaker's subject? Do you require rest? Do heat and light bother you? What other things affect you both positively and negatively?
4. Are there any mannerisms or gestures that cause you to turn off the speaker? Close your eyes and think of three mannerisms you do not like.
5. What words, phrases, or illustrations cause you to react negatively toward a person you are speaking with? One of my negatives, for instance, is when a person asks to pick my brain. The connotation is totally negative to me.
6. When listening do you generally nod or give some other form of feedback to the speaker? If you are listening carefully, think about how you act when you are listening. Likewise, think how you act when you are not listening effectively.
7. The next time you listen to a speaker, give particular attention to the opening statement and the closing. In a negotiation the first words uttered by a negotiator are very important. They set the stage for the entire negotiation.
8. The more attention you pay to body language, the better listener you can become due to your increased awareness of the other person. By studying body language, you become aware that someone is communicating a message to you prior to verbalizing it.

Speaking. Listening is only half the skill necessary to communicate effectively in a negotiation. Speaking is the other half.

Becoming an effective negotiator requires that you become an effective speaker. Recall that one of the traits of a good negotiator discussed in Chapter 9 is to be an effective speaker under stress. Practice good speaking techniques. For instance, learn to make eye contact with your audience. Understand the impact of your own dress and stature on how you talk. Take courses from Dale Carnegie or other speech therapy institutes. Subscribe to a speaking newsletter such as the Decker Communications Report (you can write for it at 607 North Sherman Avenue, Madison, WI 53704).

In your contract, be certain to cover all aspects of the issues discussed during the negotiations. You should never leave a negotiation and have to face a client later in the project who says to you "if only you had told me."

Number of Parties

Whenever there are more than two parties in a negotiation, the negotiation becomes complex. Thus when you invite subcontractors to participate in the negotiation, always contact your liability insurance carrier to find out the implications of involving other parties in the negotiation. Likewise, when your client brings in outside specialists such as attorneys or accountants, be aware that the complexities of the negotiation may become too burdensome to avoid calling in a liability specialist.

Liability is an issue that cannot be ignored, and the more hands in the negotiating process, the more difficult the liability aspects of the negotiation are to assess. By keeping the number of people in the negotiating process to a minimum, you avoid the necessity of "covering your tracks."

Bidding

Obviously, bidding for professional services has a severe impact on liability and few professional liability underwriters are interested in insuring design professionals who secure work through the bid process. They do not feel that brain surgeons, clergy, or design professionals in private practice can properly be engaged solely on that basis. Rather, it is generally their feeling that professional liability exposure created by the bid process makes it foolhardy for them to provide coverage for design professionals who gain work in this manner.

Liability underwriters believe that if a design professional prices a job too low in order to secure the project, the quality of the work will naturally suffer, leading to more liability exposure. All liability insurance carriers maintain statistics on firms; these data indicate that those who secure work primarily through shaving fees incur higher liability risk than those who secure work in other negotiated processes. If you are faced with a bid, remember that there is a potential impact on liability. Even in a negotiated contract, do not forget that liability is a concern.

If you undernegotiate any aspect of the scope and are forced to cut corners, you may be placing yourself in jeopardy for a future liability suit. As you plan for and execute the negotiation process, take steps to remember that liability is a factor to be considered by including it in every checklist. Checklists 13-1 and 13-2 provide steps for you to use to prepare for your negotiations. Note that Checklist 13-1 includes a question on the liability impact of the negotiation itself.

Constant Exposure to Liability

Whether or not you successfully negotiate your contract, you are always exposed to liability. As a design professional licensed properly in your state, you are bound to protect the health and welfare of the public. With such an awesome responsibility, do not hesitate to pursue any line of questioning in a negotiation session that helps you ferret out a further liability exposure between you and your client.

The time to ask about liability issues is at the negotiating table, not at the witness stand in a courtroom. For further information on how to deal with liability during a contract negotiation, use Table 13-1, which contains a list of all insurance carriers currently serving the design professions.

● Checklist 13-1. Points to Help You Prepare for a Negotiation

○ *Client:* _____

○ *Proposal No.:* _____

○ *Place of Negotiation:* _____

○ *Time of Negotiation:* _____

○ *Attendees:*
   A. Client's representatives (name and title/function)
   B. Firm's representatives (name and title/function)

○ *Client's Chief Negotiator:*

○ Does the client's chief negotiator have the authority to negotiate?

○ *Negotiation Agenda:*

○ *Contract Risk Analysis* (see Checklist 13-2)

○ What do we expect out of this negotiation? (objectives)

○ What are the important issues?

○ What is *our* position on these issues?

○ What do we think *their* position on these issues will be?

○ What are the alternatives?

○ Do we have the necessary facts to back up our position?

○ What are our strengths and weaknesses? What are theirs?

○ What are the questions we are going to ask them?

○ What are the questions we hope they don't ask us? Can we answer them?

○ Don't forget to listen very carefully to what they say and how they say it.

○ Be conscious of erasure words and nonverbal communication.

○ Do we need any visual aids?

○ Have we done our homework?

○ Have we planned and practiced our negotiation roles?

○ What is our walk-away price? Can we say *no*?

○ What is our liability exposure?

○ *Memo of Negotiations*

● Checklist 13-2. Contract Risk Analysis

O *Client:* _____

O *Proposal No.:* _____

O *Proposal Due Date:* _____

O *Scope of Work:* _____

O *Period of Service:* _____

O *Type of Contract:* _____

O *Amount:* _____

O *Payment Terms:* _____

O *Method of Award:* _____

O *Special Terms and Conditions:* _____

O *Remarks:* _____

O *Risks (R) and Protections (P):* _____
    (R)
    (P)

● Table 13-1. Professional Liability Insurance Companies

COMPANY	CONTACT	NOTES
Continental Casualty Co. (CNA) Victor O. Schinnerer & Co., Inc. 5028 Wisconsin Ave., N.W. Washington, DC 20016	Homer Sandridge Senior Acc't Exec. (202) 686-2850	Commended by AIA and NSPE. Available on a nationwide basis with network of claims specialists.
Lloyds of London Illinois R.B. Jones 175 West Jackson Boulevard Chicago, IL 60604	Richard A. Oldani Executive Vice Pres. M. Linda Deiss Assistant Vice Pres. (312) 435-8200	Policy is available in most states, but not all.
Insurance Co. of North America (INA) INAX 120 South Riverside Plaza Chicago, IL 60606	William B. Turner Vice President (312) 621-6448	Policies are written by either California Union or Pacific Union. Availability of policy is unknown.

Design Professional Insurance Corp. (DPIC) Union Bank Building, Suite 545 50 California Street San Francisco, CA 94111	George B. Frankforter, Jr. Vice President (415) 433-1676	Available in a handful of states, mostly on West Coast.
Northbrook Insurance Co. Shand-Morahan & Co., Inc. Shand Morahan Plaza Evanston, IL 60201	(312) 866-2800	Shand-Morahan has requested all prospects to contact their independent insurance agent only. Policy is available in most states.
International Surplus Lines Insurance Co. Professional Coverage Managers, Inc. 90 William Street New York, NY 10038	Richard C. Marx President John J. Lynch Assistant Vice Pres. (212) 344-8200	Policy is available in several states, but not all.
Imperial Casualty & Indemnity Co. Thomas F. Sheehan, Inc. 460 South Northwest Highway Park Ridge, IL 60068	Thomas Sheehan President (312) 696-3366	Policy is available in several states, but not all.

14 Government Negotiating

- How do government negotiations differ from private ones?

- How experienced are government negotiators?

- What are unallowable costs in government negotiations?

- Are there new regulations for federal government negotiations?

- What differences are there in government interpretations of regulations?

- Where can you get government regulations?

- Is CADD unallowable under government regulations?

- How can you combat government paperwork?

One of the most structured and organized types of negotiating environments is that involving a government agency. Federal government agencies are especially well organized for the entire negotiating process. Preparation by a government agency is endless even in advance of selecting the design firm that will perform the project.

Fairness is a cornerstone of the entire negotiating process in most cases. It should be noted that the government's main objective is to protect the taxpayers and to obtain a fair and equitable contract for the services provided. This is accomplished by paying no more than you would charge other similar clients in the marketplace. On the other hand, most private sector clients are driven by profit motives and thus negotiate with different objectives from the beginning.

Unfortunately, because most government agencies are bureaucratic, the intent of the law is often twisted, and many negotiations are perceived to be unfair examples of how the negotiating process can take advantage of an unprepared design professional. Use the material in this chapter to prepare yourself for a more effective government negotiation the next time you participate in one.

Understand the Different Needs of Government Employees

According to Roy A. Nierenberg, noted negotiating expert and attorney from San Francisco, government employees have a different level of needs than private sector business executives. Most business professionals are aware of their own needs; however, there is often confusion about needs on the government side. A quick review of the Nierenberg need hierarchy, which is part of his need theory,* will help you assess the needs of agencies and government officials:

❶ Homeostatic. For example, the agency has a need to maintain itself by withstanding budget cuts. Government employees are concerned with keeping their jobs and must therefore cover themselves.

❷ Safety and security. A principal need of the agency is to be secure in its mission and to enjoy continued

*Roy A. Nierenberg, "The Art of Negotiating Newsletter," vol. 2, no. 8 (May 1982).

backing to carry out its mandate.

❸ Love and belonging. The agency generally wishes to please the person in charge, that is, the President. Agency officials often also wish to extend courtesy to former employees, recognizing that the cards can be turned at a later time.

❹ Esteem. The agency wishes to be well thought of in the government community. Government employees wish to be respected by their peers.

❺ Self-actualization. Both a government agency and its employees, particularly at the higher levels, like to initiate publicly beneficial programs. They do so in large measure to achieve personal excellence.

❻ To know and understand. Agencies and many of their staff have a need to be knowledgeable about how the agency's programs will work out.

❼ Copacetic. Agency officials wish to have their programs in balance with their overall missions and goals. Some agency officials feel more comfortable with well-established and -accepted patterns.

Each negotiation should be assessed to determine how the needs of the agency and the government official involved can be satisfied. As part of your negotiation planning, spend a significant amount of time discussing the needs of the agency. Go to the agency and interview its employees. Spend time researching the history of the agency and its funding requirements. Research the purpose for the project.

As part of your research, it is important to find out the specific need for the project, whether or not a budgetary or a regulatory need is being filled. For instance, many agencies create projects to fulfill budget requirements and have no sincere need for the project. Therefore, assess how the project will be financed and where the idea for the project came from. If the idea originated outside the agency, the needs of the particular agency may be simply to administer someone else's idea. If in fact the idea comes from a strong and justifiable need within the agency, set your strategy for the negotiation appropriately. For instance, if a government building truly needs renovation, the project is real. But if an agency is spending just to justify keeping money in a future year's budget, you could face difficulties.

The needs of government employees and officials are different from private sector needs. Understand them, and it will make government negotiating more effective.

Paperwork

We are all aware that government forms are numerous and long. Table 14-1 lists just a few of the various fee proposal forms used by federal agencies. Even though the Paperwork Reduction Act under President Reagan has cut the amount of paperwork significantly, most government agencies still require elaborate forms and procedures prior to negotiations. Figure 14-1 shows the submission of a simple cost summary for a design project involving a scientific study. Note that filling out government forms involves elaborate disclosure of all internal costs and overhead items. Such paperwork requirements often negate the effectiveness of a small design firm in a government negotiation, because smaller firms do not keep elaborate records and are not able to comply with government agencies' requests for such submissions.

Although government paperwork can and often does work against you, there are situations in which it can work *for* you. For instance, keep in mind that should a sharp negotiator fail to arrive at an effective agreement with you when you have been chosen as the first design team in a selection procedure, that contract negotiator will have to fill out a substantial amount of paperwork to justify why he or she has gone to the second firm in the procedure. The fact that the paperwork is a burden on the government employee provides an incentive for that individual to success-fully negotiate with you. Such a factor could make the difference in your next negotiation.

Importance of Preparation

Unlike many private sector negotiations, the government employs teams of design professionals to prepare elaborate cost estimates and scope definitions for each project that will go through the selection procedure.

● **Table 14-1. List of Fee Proposal Forms Used by Various Federal Government Agencies**

Form	User Agencies
DD Form 633-1 Contract Pricing Proposal (Technical Services)	Corps of Engineers, Naval Facilities Engineering Command, and the National Aeronautics and Space Administration
NAVFAC 11012/2 (5-75) A&E Fee Proposal	Atlantic Division, Naval Facilities Engineering Command, and the Officer-in-Charge of Construction, Trident
14ND PACDIV 04-11012/1 (3-76) A&E Proposal	Pacific Division, Naval Facilities Engineering Command
12ND WESTDIV 11012/1 (Rev. 6-78) A&E Fee Itemization	Western Division, Naval Facilities Engineering Command
GSA Form 2630 (2-71) Architect-Engineer Cost Estimate	General Services Administration—all regions
GSA Form 2631 (2-71) Architect-Engineer Cost Estimate Summary	General Services Administration—all regions
Form FEC 4-17 (7-78) A/E Fee Proposal Breakdown	Department of Health and Human Services
Form FEC 4-18 (7-78) A/E Fee Proposal Summary	Department of Health and Human Services
VA Form 08-6298 (May 1976) Architect-Engineer Fee Proposal	Veterans Administration
Professional Services Estimate Work Sheets (no form number)	U.S. Postal Service
Schedule of Designated Services (no form number)	Department of State
Optional Form 60 (Research and Development)	San Francisco Operations Office, Department of Energy, and Ames Research Center, National Aeronautics and Space Administration
Architect-Engineer Cost Estimate (no form number)	Department of Energy (optional form)

● Figure 14-1. Cost Summary

PART II. COST SUMMARY				TOTALS
7. DIRECT LABOR *(Specify labor categories)*	EST. HOURS	HOURLY RATE	ESTIMATED COST	
E VI Senior Agricultural Engineers,		$	$	
Geologists and Economists	320	13.25	4,240	
E V Project Managers	1,048	12.00	12,575	
E III Planner, Economist, Geologist,				
Environmental Scientist, Hydrologist	1,672	9.00	15,050	
T III Technicians	312	6.90	2,155	
T II Technicians	232	5.80	1,345	
Office	376	4.30	1,615	
DIRECT LABOR TOTAL:				$ 36,980
8. INDIRECT COSTS *(Specify indirect cost pools)*	RATE	RATE BASE	ESTIMATED COST	
Salary overheads @ 30% of Direct Labor		$	$ 11,095	
General and administrative overheads				
@ 100% of direct labor			36,980	
INDIRECT COSTS TOTAL:				$ 48,075
9. OTHER DIRECT COSTS				
a. TRAVEL	NO. OF MAN TRIPS	COST PER MAN TRIP	ESTIMATED COST	
LONG DISTANCE		$	$	
LOCAL				
See attached detail			2,905	
PER DIEM	NO. DAYS	RATE PER DAY	ESTIMATED COST	
See attached detail		$	$ 1,945	
TRAVEL SUBTOTAL:			$ 4,850	
b. EQUIPMENT, MATERIALS, SUPPLIES *(Specify categories)*	QTY	COST	ESTIMATED COST	
Printing and reproduction - see attached		$	$	
detail			2,940	
EQUIPMENT SUBTOTAL:			$ 2,940	
c. SUBCONTRACTS			ESTIMATED CO COSTS	
Archeological consultant			$ 3,750	
SUBCONTRACTS SUBTOTAL:			$ 3,750	
d. OTHER *(Specify categories)*			ESTIMATED COST	
			$	
OTHER SUBTOTAL			$	
OTHER DIRECT COSTS TOTAL:				$ 11,540
10. TOTAL ESTIMATED COST				$ 96,595
11. PROFIT				
a. PROFIT TOTAL				$ 14,500
		b. 15	% OF COST	
12. TOTAL PRICE				$ 111,095

*Roy A. Nierenberg, "The Art of Negotiating Newsletter," vol. 2, no. 8 (May 1982).

Item #7   DETAIL

TASKS AND MAN-DAY REQUIREMENTS

TASKS	Office	T-2	T-3	E-3	E-5	E-6
1. Environmental Setting	10	5	3			
A. Natural Environment				30	10	2
B. Human Related Environment				16	6	4
2. Preliminary Draft Report						
A. Narrative	5			26	8	
B. Graphics		3	2			
C. Consultant Review						3
D. Printing						
E. Client Review				2	2	
3. Community Involvement						
A. News Releases	1				2	
B. Questionnaires	1	3	2	6	4	1
C. Workshops	2	2	6	7	7	2
D. Public Hearings	2	2	4	3	5	2
4. Client Management Program						
A. Program Description	2	2	2	17	12	1
B. Program Alternatives	4	2	4	30	16	2
5. Probable Environmental Impacts						
A. Impacts (Primary, Secondary, Unavoidable)	5	2	3	30	25	5
B. Mitigations	2		1	10	8	3
C. Short Term vs. Long Term	2		1	5	3	1
D. Irreversible Commitment of Resources	2		1	5	3	1
6. Draft Environmental Report						
A. Narrative	6			12	10	4
B. Graphics		8	10			
C. Consultant Review						4
D. Client Review					2	
7. Comments and Response (Draft Report)	3			10	8	5
8. EIS Final Report (Client Responsibility)						
Days	47	29	39	209	131	40
Hours	376	232	312	1672	1048	320

Item #8 DETAIL

Salary Overheads	Total as % of Direct Labor	Unallowable Costs as a % of Direct Labor	Allowable Costs as a % of Direct Labor
Payroll Taxes	8.2	–	8.2
Paid Leaves	13.6	–	13.6
Group Insurance	5.2	–	5.2
Pension Plan	3.0	–	3.0
Total Salary Overheads	30.0	–	30.0

General and Administrative Overheads

	Total as % of Direct Labor	Unallowable Costs as a % of Direct Labor	Allowable Costs as a % of Direct Labor
Indirect Salaries	31.1	–	36.1
Incentive Pay	12.3	–	12.3
Buildings and Equipment	16.4	–	16.4
Licenses and Insurance	6.4	–	6.4
Professional Services	7.0	.1	6.9
Travel and Subsistence	7.9	.3	7.6
Supplies and Interest	8.6	1.4	7.2
Professional Education	1.6	–	1.6
Recruiting Costs	2.1	–	2.1
Printing	3.4	–	3.4
Contributions	.2	.2	–
Bad Debts	.5	.5	–
	102.5	2.5	100.0

Item #9a. DETAIL

TRAVEL AND PER DIEM

TASKS	Days	Persons	1. Vehicles	2. Airfare	3. Per Diem
Baseline Inventories	28	2	710	500	860
Review of Preliminary Draft	4	2	100	100	120
Community Involvement Meetings	12	2	310	300	380
Analysis of Client Program	10	1	255	100	330
Impact Analysis	5	1	130	100	155
Draft EIS Report Review	2	1	50	100	50
Comments & Response Review	2	1	50	100	50
			Total $ 2,905		$ 1,945

Notes:

1. Rental car at $17 per day and $0.17 per mile, Est. 50 miles per day.

2. Estimated plane fare round trip.

3. Per diem at $35 per day, $20 per person subtracted from total per staff-trip for last day's lodging expenses.

Item #9b. DETAIL

PRINTING AND REPRODUCTION

Preliminary Report - (10 copies, 8-1/2" x 11")
Narrative format. Graphics and illustrative materials
will be in preliminary format only. Black and white
print, 50 sheets. $ 240

Draft Environmental Report - (50 copies, 8-1/2" x 11")
Narrative format. Graphics will be in finalized format
with approximately 10 foldouts. Black and white print,
125 sheets. $ 2,500

Comment & Response Report - 10 copies, 8-1/2" x 11")
Narrative format. Black and white print, 50 sheets. $ 200

                                    Total Cost $ 2,940
                                                           ======

Thus, by the time you arrive at the negotiation session to determine the fee for the project, the government has already studied the project in great detail for months. Without adequate preparation by your design team for the negotiation, you will undoubtedly lose, simply because the government has more information. Therefore whenever planning to negotiate with the government, increase your preparation time appropriately. Investigate all angles of scope and schedule versus cost and be able to substantiate every figure that you quote to a government negotiator. It makes no sense whatsoever to enter any government negotiation without preparation. You will undoubtedly lose.

No Loss Leaders

There is always a temptation with a new client to do a job at a "lower" fee to prove to the client you are so good that they will select you for the next project. Such "loss leaders" are not effective with most government clients since they are bound to select design firms by the fairest possible method for each project. Because you lost money on a prior project, you are not automatically guaranteed one in the future. Also, those responsible for the selection of a design firm do not negotiate and vice versa.

Undoubtedly we are all tempted to do loss leaders, but in the government arena do not enter a negotiation with the concept of a loss leader on your mind or you may regret winning the job in the first place. It is much more effective to win a job fairly and to negotiate a win-win contract than to attempt to persuade a client negotiator that you should obtain the next project on the basis of reducing your fee on this one. In fact, chances you will negotiate with the same individual on the next government contract are very slim.

Allowable and Unallowable Costs

The most controversial area in government negotiating is the area of allowable and unallowable costs under federal government procurement regulations. Effective April 1, 1984, the U.S. federal government enacted the Federal Acquisition Regulation (FAR) that replaces all federal procurement regulations covering design contracts prior to April 1, 1984. The specific paragraph in FAR is part 31, and it replaces old Defense Acquisition Regulations (DAR), Section 15, and Federal Procurement Regulations (FPR), part 15. There are several significant differences between the new FAR law and the older FPR. The new law attempts to separate design professionals even further from construction contractors and facility contracts. An attempt is made in the new regulation to support the Brooks Bill* which is a bill protecting design professionals from price competition as a sole selection criterion. However, there are significant differences in the new bill that can be detrimental to a design firm.

In a presentation in June 1984 before the Professional Services Management Association in Chicago, government contracting expert Edwin P. James, principal of the government contract division of Arthur Anderson and Company in Chicago, presented a list of unallowable costs that are currently hot topics under federal government audits of design firms. Figure 14-2 lists those costs. In addition, he described a list of 40 gray area costs that are often questioned by federal government auditors. These can be found in Figure 14-3.

Unallowable costs are those that are not allowed to be carried with a design firm's overhead. The biggest contention of most design professionals is that many of these costs are necessary business operations. However, the federal government has maintained the position over the past two decades that any unallowable costs such as interest or entertainment should not be paid for by federal government clients because they are not benefiting by the expenditures.

A major difficulty arises when the government auditor who reviews your financial records has never dealt with a design firm before. Since government auditors are generally young, anyone who has not dealt with a design firm is not aware of the many subtleties in operating such a business. For this reason unallowable costs are often disputed by design profes-

*The Brooks Bill is U.S. Public Law #92-582, which was enacted on Oct. 27, 1972.

● Figure 14-2. Unallowable Costs

Compensation for Personal Services

  Excessive by element

  Severance payments

  Banked vacations

  Stock plans for executives

  Supplemental retirement plans

  Pension accruals

  Uncompensated overtime

Warranties

Lobbying Expense

  (Political Advocacy)

Defense of Fraud Proceedings

10 Percent Withholding on

  Cost Accounting Standards (CAS)

Relocation Costs

Selling Costs (Foreign Sales)

Goodwill

Equal Access to Justice Act

Overseas Employees Income Tax

  (including preparation fees)

Spare Parts

Tax Legislation (research

  and development credit

  and completed contract accounting)

Health Care Cost Containment

Teleconferencing

Examination of Contractor

  Records of Unclaimed Costs

● Figure 14-3. Gray Area Costs Questioned

1. Excessive executive compensation.
2. Rent between closely held companies.
3. Overhead and general and administrative (G&A) expense rates.
4. Single overhead rate (including G&A expense).
5. Field overhead rate.
6. Direct versus indirect charging.
7. Idle capacity and facilities.
8. Legal costs.
9. First class air travel
10. Employee moving allowance.
11. Industrial research and development (IR&D) and business and plant (B&P) expense.
12. Organization costs.
13. Losses on other contracts.
14. Patent costs.
15. Fines and penalties.
16. Plant reconversion costs.
17. Ownership costs versus rental costs.
18. Royalties.
19. Selling costs.
20. State and local taxes (federal income tax is unallowable).
21. Base for indirect rates.
22. Allocability of costs.
23. Reasonableness of costs.
24. Cost accounting standards (CAS) violations.
25. Unpaid overtime.
26. Special termination costs.
27. Company-owned aircraft.
28. Contingencies in bid.
29. Business development expense.
30. Treatment of direct labor fringes.
31. Bonuses and incentive compensation.
32. Pension costs.
33. Labor utilization.
34. Defective pricing.
35. Unabsorbed fixed overhead in claims.
36. Deferred compensation.
37. Lobbying expense.
38. Fraud.
39. Goodwill.
40. Directly associated costs.

sionals in contract negotiations. Be prepared to justify your entire position on allowable versus unallowable costs and also be prepared to question the findings of an auditor in a preaudit, precontract-audit situation. Do not simply take the word of an auditor without putting up a fight.

CADD versus Productivity. One of the most controversial and debatable unallowable costs in today's marketplace is the use of computer-aided design and drafting (CADD) equipment by design professionals. Many government agencies are taking the position that computer-aided design and drafting equipment is an unallowable cost for government work because they say that design professionals minimize the use of such equipment on government work and maximize it on private sector work. In addition, the cost of such equipment is high, and the government does not want to pay market prices for any service that could be bought at a lower cost. As a result of the government's intense investigation into the cost factors associated with computer-aided drafting, one Florida design firm has initiated a policy of using their CADD equipment only on private sector work and using manpower on all other government-related projects. To counter this, a 68-page report encouraging government agencies to use design firms that have CADD equipment was published in 1980 (see Selected Bibliography).

It is ironic that the federal government should question the cost of tools designed to improve the productivity of design work and that in fact reduce overall design fees to the client. Yet in most agencies this is the case. It is even more ironic that many federal agencies now require specific CADD systems by design firms that are selected to do work, while their negotiating counterparts eliminate the cost reimbursement for the very equipment demanded by the client. Only through years of persuasion in negotiations can design professionals return to compensation based on results. Using lump-sum agreements begins to pave the way for such persuasion.

Lump-Sums Always

With federal, state, and local government clients it is important to always seek lump-sum agreements. Lump-sum agreements can avoid the necessity of audit procedures prior to your contract and avoid an audit after the contract in most cases. It makes sense to even provide an incentive to your client to agree to a lump sum by reducing your fee 5 percent if the client will agree to it.

Lump-sum contracts are easier to administer. Invoices are more simple. Paperwork is reduced, and you are provided an incentive for performing the work more efficiently. Therefore, lump-sum contracts benefit both the client and the design professional by providing such an incentive.

Brainstorm a series of benefits to convince even the most stubborn of government clients that a lump-sum contract is "the way to go." Be certain that the benefits reflect both your perspective and your client's perspective so that a win-win agreement can be kept in mind at all times.

Never Redesign

Once you have established your scope of work for any government project, never redesign the project without being compensated for it as an extra service. Government negotiators and government clients are notorious for asking a design professional to make changes on a project once the agreement is set. Read your agreement carefully, and communicate it to all the members of your design team so that everyone knows exactly what is expected by the government client and what will be paid for.

We hear constantly of design firms that lose on government contracts only to find that they have continually changed the scope of services without the approval of the client. Never make changes without specific written orders from the client. Also investigate and learn the government change order procedure so that your staff may be efficient at processing design work change orders. Each agency has a different procedure, which your firm should be fully aware of prior to starting the work.

Get Paid in Advance

Whenever possible ask for a retainer in advance from the federal or any local government. If you are providing a substantive service, such a retainer can offset the loss of unallowable costs in your overhead by providing interest earnings to the firm. One design firm in Houston, Texas, was able to secure a 50 percent advance payment on a Housing and Urban Development (HUD) project by asking for it in the negotiation as compensation for lost revenue due to unallowable costs deducted from the firm's multiplier. Although it was difficult to obtain, the negotiating officer finally released the money in an escrow account on which the interest would be paid to the design professional.

The surest way never to obtain a payment in advance is never to ask for it. Always attempt to secure payments in advance with both private and public clients.

The 6 Percent Fee Limit

Most design professionals believe that the fee limit identified in federal government regulations as the maximum fee for design services is in fact the maximum fee for any work performed on the project. However, this is not true. The 6 percent fee limit covers only the design work on the project; design work can be defined as the time the designer puts into "designing" the project for the government. Specifically excluded from this 6 percent fee limit are many items such as field trips, sight inspection, project meetings, construction observation, preparation of bid documents, preparation of estimates, and preparation of reports.

Be certain when negotiating with the government that you do not allow government regulations to defeat you without knowing exactly what they say. Instead obtain a copy of all pertinent government regulations that cover your design projects and read them carefully. Anyone who has read the government language with regard to the 6 percent fee limit is able to find ways to obtain higher fees on a project. In fact one Florida firm made a 22.4 percent fee on a $1.2 million post office project in 1982. Only through a complete understanding of change order procedures and the 6 percent fee regulation was this firm able to obtain such a fee. If your firm has been restricted to 6 percent fees because of a lack of understanding of proper regulations, take the time now to upgrade your information.

Cost Data

More than ever, substantial cost data are important to government negotiations. As mentioned in earlier chapters you should obtain current copies of all surveys to substantiate any cost data that you are providing to a government client. Remember, when sitting in a negotiation with a government client, it is vital that you provide the latest cost data to substantiate your figures. The use of two-year-old cost data can easily be argued against by a government negotiator who could probably provide you with the latest figures based on currently available government surveys of design firms.

When using cost data be careful not to "sink your own ship" by not understanding the implications of the data that you use. Study surveys carefully to determine how all figures were assembled and how they were analyzed prior to quoting them in a government negotiation. Also understand what cost data are available from the government itself by placing your firm on a government publication list; simply contact any U.S. government printing office or the main office in Pueblo, Colorado.

Most government agencies require specific accounting procedures to be followed before the negotiation as well as substantiation of three or four years' history of your figures. Be certain that your accountant and bookkeeper understand the ramifications of entering a negotiation with a new government client. Often a bookkeeping system must be completely revamped to provide the information needed for a particular negotiation. Only you can judge if it is worth your time and effort to do so with a government client.

Your First Government Negotiation?

If you are about to enter your first government negotiation, there are three primary considerations to remember when negotiating any government contract:

❶ Remember that negotiating is not a contest. A win-win strategy is the optimum strategy in most design firm negotiations, and you should attempt to restructure your tactics to achieve a win-win for a repeat client and a mutually satisfying agreement.

❷ Never fail to negotiate no matter how great your differences appear. Remember that time is a great healer and that the more is invested in a negotiation the more likely the outcome will be a win-win.

❸ Train your people in negotiating techniques. More than ever government clients spend an inordinate amount of hours training skilled negotiators. Remember that every hour of training can be rewarded by a substantial amount of dollars won at the negotiating table. Take the time now to assess your firm's strengths and weaknesses in negotiating and improve any weaknesses through adequate training programs.

Checklist 14-1 lists the ten primary reasons for failure in negotiating. Review each of the reasons with your staff and identify whether or not you have failed

---

● **Checklist 14-1. Ten Primary Reasons for Failure in Negotiation**

○ Poor listening.
○ Few questions asked.
○ Very seldom a disclosure.
○ Don't separate fact finding from negotiating.
○ Semantic difficulties.
○ Close door on alternatives.
○ Prospective problems negatively affect the person.
○ Very little recap.
○ Limits too quickly established.
○ Teams don't use all members.

---

at negotiating during the past six months because of any of them.

Remember, an effective negotiator never stops learning. Train yourself to be a better negotiator, and then train others in your firm to follow in your footsteps. Finally, use my own personal list of 21 tips on negotiating (Checklist 14-2) to improve every negotiation you face in the future.

● **Checklist 14-2. Stasiowski's 21 Tips on Negotiations**

○ Have a compelling desire to win (Vince Lombardi said, "Winning is the only thing").

○ Learn how to negotiate.

○ Make your own luck but have some.

○ Negotiate only with those in authority.

○ Satisfy the needs of *all* parties; negotiations mean win-win not win-lose.

○ Make an early concession.

○ Be prepared to trade.

○ Be calm.

○ Sell.

○ Don't compromise your objectives.

○ Deal from strength.

○ Tell your story yourself.

○ Don't oversell.

○ Keep a poker face.

○ Don't underestimate others.

○ Be personal.

○ Respect confidentiality.

○ Be confident.

○ Be reasonable.

○ Be flexible.

○ Always end on a positive note.

 # Sources of Comparative Financial Statistics

Annual Statement Studies. Latest Edition. Robert Morris Associates, Philadelphia, PA. (Also available in many business libraries.)

Comparative Financial Summary of Publicly Held Companies Engaged in Construction and Related Activities. V. B. Castellani & Co., Inc., Latest Edition. Available from V. B. Castellani & Co., Inc., 251 Commonwealth Avenue, Boston, MA 02116.

Compensation Guidelines for Architectural and Engineering Services. 1981. Available from the AIA.

Compensation Management: A Guide for Small Firms. Peter Piven, AIA. 1982. Available from the AIA.

Financial Analysis of Engineering, Architectural and Surveying Services (SIC 8911). Dun & Bradstreet, Inc., 1981. Available from Dun & Bradstreet, Inc., and also found in many business libraries. (Earlier editions also available.)

Financial Management for Architects. Robert F. Mattox, 1980. Available from the AIA.

Financial Management for the Design Professional. Lowell V. Getz & Frank A. Stasiowski. Whitney Library of Design, New York, NY, 1984. Also available for $32.95 from PSMJ, 126 Harvard Street, Brookline, MA 02146.

Financial Management and Project Control for Consulting Engineers. Lowell V. Getz. 1983. ACEC publication no. 52.

1984 Executive Management Salary Survey. *Professional Services Management Journal,* 1984. Available for $80 from PSMJ, 126 Harvard Street, Brookline, MA 02146.

1983 Executive Management Salary Survey. *Professional Services Management Journal,* 1983. Available for $10 from PSMJ, 126 Harvard Street, Brookline, MA 02146.

1983 Operating Statistics for Professional Firms. Harper and Shuman, Inc., 68 Moulton Street, Cambridge, MA 02138.

1983 Salary and Marketing Expense Survey. Society for Marketing Professional Services and A/E Marketing Journal (out of print). New edition available from SMPS, 1437 Powhatan Street, Alexandria, VA 22314.

1982 Financial Statistics Survey for Professional Service Firms. *Professional Services Management Journal,* 1982. Available for $10 from PSMJ, Post Office Box 11316, Newington, CT 06111.

"A Painless System for Uniform Cost Accounting." Donald J. Smally, *Consulting Engineer,* June 1978.

Professional Services Management Journal. Various issues. Contact Michael Hough, Publisher, PSMJ, Post Office Box 11316, Newington, CT 06111.

Standardized Accounting for Architects. Robert F. Mattox. AIA, 1982. Available from the American Institute of Architects, 1735 New York Avenue, N.W., Washington, DC 20006.

Successful Cost Reduction Programs for Engineers and Managers. E. A. Criner, 1984. VanNostrand Reinhold & Co., 135 West 50th Street, New York, NY 10020.

A Survey of Management Control Practices in Large Architectural/Engineering Firms. James S. Reece. The University of Michigan, Graduate School of Business Administration, Ann Arbor, MI 48104.

Other Sources: Various issues of *AIA Journal, Architectural Record, Consulting Engineer, Progressive Architecture,* and limited data available from the various professional societies.

Salary Surveys: Various salary survey statistics are available from many AIA chapters and from the Society for Marketing Professional Services.

Building Block Agreement

Instructions for Preparing Building Block Agreement for a Designated Services Project Excerpted from an Agreement Created by King & King Architects, Syracuse, New York.

1. Review the General Descriptions and form of Agreement utilizing preliminary knowledge of the project and type of owner to formulate an approach to developing the scope of services at the initial meetings with the Owner.

2. Meet with the Owner and determine project requirements as completely as possible. Include consultants in the meeting if appropriate.

3. Based on the information gathered, prepare a contract.

   a. The basic terms of the AIA Owner/Architect Agreement Articles 1 thru 3 should be fairly constant.

   b. Scope of Service Forms (Exhibit A) should be completed and a set of General Descriptions (Exhibit B) created to suit the situation. Define which consultant performs which services on scope outline forms.

   c. Meet with consultants to verify their understanding of the scope of their work. Request a fee proposal by project phase and a not-to-exceed total from the consultant, including contingencies, in writing. This fee quote is in dollars, not hours. Also request consultant to prepare General Description for the services he/she is to provide.

   d. Carry out a similar process with each internal department involved in the work. Modified scope outlines are useful as worksheets for organizing manhour estimates by job category by service. Request hours and dollars from each discipline. Determine whether those figures include contingencies.

   e. Review each fee quote with the person submitting it to verify understanding of scope.

   f. Prepare a total fee estimate by adding all individual estimates together. Utilize a contingency, if necessary, to establish a not-to-exceed figure.

   g. Once reviewed and approved by the Project Administration team, the contract shall be reviewed by the Management Council for conformity to overall firm policy.

h. A minimum of 3 copies are required, all signed; one remains in our file for reference, two are furnished to the Owner for signature with a request that one executed copy be returned to us and one retained for his file.

4. Do not prepare any kind of formal fee quote to an Owner without first obtaining, in writing, a fee quote from consultants.

5. Do not sign a contract with consultants or authorize any work until the Owner/Architect Agreement is signed.

6. The key to this type of Agreement for "Designated Services" is the *definition of each service to be provided.* These are created for each job using guideline General Descriptions. Please give careful attention to the following notes on preparing scope definitions.

7. At each General Description the Preparer must answer the following questions:

   a. Is the item required? Services not to be provided shall be so stated in the general descriptions "Not to be provided."

   b. Scope item heading . . . is it the correct terminology?

   c. Is the item required on the form described in the *guide definition* or in a modified service?

   d. Who provides the service?

   e. What is the description of the actual services to be provided in this case?

   f. Is there standard language desired by us if a particular service is selected?

   g. Is there nonstandard language which is to be modified for each job?

   h. Is the service known to be required but indefinite at this time? How to handle?

   i. Is it a service we desire the Owner provide because our liability insurance does not cover us for the exposure?

   j. What is the effect on other sections of definition created in this section?

   k. Is it a service we need to perform in order to retain proper control?

8. Contract scope definition should state detailed conditions on which price is based. For example: If public presentations are anticipated but the number is not known, the definition should state the number of presentations upon which the estimated fee is based.

9. For all services to be provided by the Owner whether provided by him or separate consultants, *the Architect needs to be sure he/she understands the scope of work the Owner intends to perform.* His understanding should be documented in the general description to avoid later misunderstanding, gaps, and overlaps in service.

10. The final General Description created for a given job should *not* include obviously ambiguous words or phases such as *usually, normally, may include, traditionally, if authorized, if required, if, may.*

11. On certain projects, it may not initially be possible to outline the Scope of Services for all Phases. Following are suggested modifications in order to accomplish this and add scope definitions and fee quotations by amendment at a later date:

a. Add Paragraphs 1.1.2 and 1.1.3 to Article 1:

    1.1.2   Exhibit Form A1, Pre-Design, has been completed for the Scope of Services defined to date. When the Project is approved to proceed, the remaining Forms A2 through A7 will be completed, as provided for in Exhibit B1.04, and attached to this Agreement.

    1.1.3   Exhibit B, General Descriptions, have been completed for the Scope of Services defined to date, the Pre-Design Phase. The General Descriptions will be completed for the remaining phases when the Project is approved, as provided for in Exhibit B1.04, and attached to this Agreement.

b. Add Paragraphs 2.1.1.3 and 2.1.1.4 to Article 2:

    2.1.1.3   For all services to be provided under Phase 1 of this Agreement, payments shall not exceed —————.

    2.1.1.4   For all services to be provided under Phases 2 through 7 of this Agreement, payments shall be determined and agreed to when the Scope of Services is defined.

12.   If a multiple of Direct Personnel Expense (DPE) is to be used instead of Billing Rates (Paragraph 2.1.1.1), the definition of DPE should be inserted in Paragraph 2.4.

    2.4.3   Direct Personnel Expense is defined as the salaries of professional, technical and clerical employees engaged on the Project by the Architect, and the cost of their mandatory and customary benefits such as statutory employee benefits, insurance, sick leave, holidays, vacations, pensions, and similar benefits.

and the words "multiple of _____ times Direct Personnel Expense" inserted in place of "hourly at the billing rates" in Paragraph 2.1.1.1.

Building Block Agreement Between Architect and Consultant for Designated Services

This Agreement

made this _____ day of _____ in the year nineteen hundred and _____

Between the **Architect**   **(Name)**
                                  (Address)

and the **Consultant**   **(Name)**
                                  (Address)

for the following Project
(Project Name,
Number and brief description
from O/A Agreement)

The Architect has made an Agreement dated _____
with the **Owner**   **(Name)**
                                (Address)

which is hereafter referred to as the Prime Agreement and which provides for furnishing Professional Services in connection with the Project described therein. A copy of Exhibit A, Scope of Services, and Exhibit B, General Descriptions, of the Prime Agreement is attached, and made a part hereof.

The **Architect** and the **Consultant** agree to the following points:

Article 1. Scope of Services
1.1   Services to Be Furnished
1.2   Additional Services
1.3   The Consultant's Responsibilities
1.4   The Architect's Responsibilities

Article 2. Payments to the Consultant
2.1   Compensation for Services
2.2   Compensation for Additional Services
2.3   Reimbursable Expenses
2.4   Method of Payment
2.5   Time of Agreement
2.6   Suspension, Abandonment, Termination

Article 3. General Terms
3.1   Engineer's Records
3.2   Termination of Agreement
3.3   Ownership of Documents
3.4   Insurance
3.5   Successors and Assigns
3.6   Arbitration
3.7   Extent of Agreement
3.8   Governing Law

Article 4. Other Conditions
4.1   Exhibit A, Scope of Service Forms
4.2   Exhibit B, General Descriptions

Architect
(Name)
By _____
     (Name), Partner
     Registration No. _____, (State)

Date _____

Consultant
(Company Name)
By _____
     (Name & Title)
     Registration No. _____, (State)
     (If Applicable)

Date _____

Suggested Modifications to Owner-Design Professional Agreement and General Conditions

by Paul M. Lurie, Esq.
Lurie, Sklar & Simon, Ltd.
180 N. Michigan Ave.
Suite 2000
Chicago, IL 60601

1. Limit of Liability (A/E Agreements)

The Architect/Engineer (A/E) will maintain for a period of one year after completion of the Project, an "errors and omissions" insurance policy in the amount of (the agreed amount of insurance) in the aggregate to protect against errors or omissions in connection with the Architect/Engineer's duties under this Agreement. The Owner agrees to look solely to the amounts available under said policy for any claims arising out of, in connection with, or resulting from work under this Agreement; and the Architect/Engineer shall have no liability (direct or indirect) to the Owner for any alleged errors, omissions, or other claims except to the extent of the said insurance proceeds.

This limitation of liability shall not apply to the extent that the professional liability carrier issuing said policy refuses coverage because of a policy defense other than one relating to the amount of coverage. Said insurance shall be evidenced by a Certificate of Insurance issued to the Owner which shall provide that said policy shall not be cancelled except upon 30 days written notice to Owner.

2. Indemnity Where Owner Has Conflict of Interest with Contractor (A/E Agreement)

(a) Owner will require all prime contractors to execute indemnification agreements holding the Owner, the Architect, the Engineer and their agents and employees harmless as set forth in the latest edition of the General Conditions of the Contract for Construction published by the American Institute of Architects (or the National Society of Professional Engineers).

(b) The Owner may choose to act as its own general contractor or may choose to instruct a contractor to deviate from the Contract Documents. Therefore, Owner hereby indemnifies and holds harmless the Architect/Engineer, its employees and consultants from and against all claims, damages, losses and expenses, including but not limited to attorneys' fees, arising out of, in connection with, or resulting from the performance of any construction where there has been a deviation from any document prepared by the Architect/Engineer or where there has been a failure to follow any written recommendation of the Architect/Engineer. In the event that Architect/Engineer or any other party indemnified hereunder is required to bring an action to enforce the provisions of this indemnity, the indemnifying party shall pay the attorneys' fees and costs incurred by the indemnified party in bringing that action.

3. Limit to Avoid Incorporation of Responsibility by Reference (Supplementary General Condition)

Where any specification which is incorporated herein by reference, through the works "and/or as directed by the Architect," or phrases having a similar effect appear to give the Architect/Engineer the right to direct something other than that specified, the Architect/Engineer has in fact *no* such right to except as it may be established in specific instances in portions of Project Manual other than in said specifications.

4. Shop Drawing Limit (Supplementary General Condition)

(a) The contractor may submit to the Architect/Engineer shop drawings, samples, and product data for the Architect/Engineer's review. These documents shall detail the equipment, material, and fabrication which contractor intends to utilize in connection with the performance of the Work. The Architect/Engineer's review of these submittals is only for conformance with the design concept of the work and is not intended to be exhaustive; nor is the Architect/Engineer obligated to verify dimensions, quantities, or the performance of any systems. The Architect/Engineer's review of a specific item shall not be considered approval of an assembly of which the item is a part.

(b) Contractor further agrees that if deviations, discrepancies, or conflict between shop drawings, samples and product data and the contract documents in the form of design drawings and specifications are discovered either prior to or after submittals are processed by the Architect/Engineer, the design drawings and specifications control and shall be followed.

5. General Condition Indemnity Replacing AIA, A-201, Sec. 4.18 and EJCDC 1910-8, Sec. 6.30-6.32

(a) To the fullest extent permitted by law, the Contractor shall indemnify and hold harmless the Owner and the Architect/Engineer and their agents and employees from and against all claims, damages, losses and expenses, including but not limited to attorneys' fees, arising out of or resulting from or in connection with the performance of the Work, provided that any such claim, damage, loss, or expense is caused in whole or in part by any negligent act or omission of the Contractor, any Subcontractor, anyone directly or indirectly employed by any of them or anyone for whose acts any of them may be liable, regardless of whether or not it is caused in part by a party indemnified hereunder. Such obligation shall not be construed to negate, abridge, or otherwise reduce any other right or obligation of indemnity or contribution which would otherwise exist as to any party or person described in this agreement.

(b) In any and all claims against the Owner or the Architect/Engineer or any of their agents or employees by any employee of the Contractor, any Subcontractor, anyone directly or indirectly employed by any of them or anyone for whose acts any of them may be liable, the indemnification obligation under this Paragraph agreement shall not be limited in any way by any limitation on the amount or type of damages, compensation or benefits payable by or for the Contractor or any Subcontractor under workers' or workmen's compensation acts, disability benefit acts or other employee benefit acts.

(c) "Claims, damages, losses, and expenses" as these words are used in this agreement shall be construed to include, but not limited to (1) injury or damage consequent upon the failure of or use or misuse by Contractor, its subcontractors, agents, servants, or employees, of any hoist, rigging, blocking, scaffolding, or any and all other kinds of items of equipment, including those covered in the Illinois Structural Work Act whether or not the same be owned, furnished, or loaned by Owner; and (2) all attorney's fees and costs incurred in bringing an action to enforce the provisions of this indemnity or any other indemnity contained in the General Conditions, as modified by the Supplementary General Conditions.

(d) Only to the extent prohibited by the Illinois Anti-Indemnity Act, Ill. Rev. Stat. C. *29*, Sec. *61* the obligations of the Contractor under this agreement shall not extend to the liability of the owner, Architect/Engineer, their agents or employees, arising out of their negligence.

6. Limit on Contractor's Right to Make Direct Claims on A/E (Supplementary General Condition)

In performing its obligations for the Owner, the Architect/Engineer and its consultants may cause expense for the Contractor or its subcontractor. However, Contractor, its subcontractors and sureties shall maintain no direct action against Architect/Engineer, its consultants, their agents and employees, for any claim arising out of, in connection with or resulting from the Work performed or required to be performed. Only the Owner shall be the beneficiary of any undertaking by the Architect/Engineer, its consultants, their agents and employees.

Only the owner shall be the beneficiary of any undertaking by the Architect/Engineer, its consultants and employees.

7. Arbitration Remedy after Completion

The remedy of arbitration shall govern all claims, disputes, and other matters in question notwithstanding the completion of construction.

Selected Bibliography

Books

Allport-Vernon. *Studies in Expressive Movement.* New York: Hafner Publishing Company, 1967.

Berne, Eric. *Games People Play.* New York: Grove Press, 1964.

Birdwhistell, Ray L. *Kinesics in Contest.* Philadelphia: University of Pennsylvania Press, 1970.

Carnegie, Dale. *How to Win Friends and Influence People.* New York: Simon & Schuster, 1981.

Coffin, Royce A. *Negotiator: A Manual For Winners.* New York: American Management Association, 1975.

David, Keith. *Human Behavior at Work.* New York: McGraw-Hill, 1971.

Davis, Flora. *Inside Intuition.* New York: Signet, 1971.

Fast, Julius. *Body Language.* New York: Evans & Company, 1970.

Feldman, Sandor S. *Mannerisms of Speech & Gestures in Everyday Life.* New York: International Universities Press, 1959.

Goffman, Ervine. *Behavior in Public Places.* New York: Mcmillian, 1963.

Gross, Harry. *How to Do Business with the Government.* New York: Pilot Books (Better Business Book Series), 1963.

Hall, E. T. *The Silent Language.* New York: Fawcett Publications, 1959.

Harris, Thomas A., M.D. *I'm O.K.—You're O.K.* New York: Avon Books, 1969.

Hinde, Robert A. *Non-Verbal Communication.* New York: Cambridge University Press, 1972.

James-Jongeward. *Born to Win.* Boston: Addison-Wesley Publishing, 1971.

Karras, Dr. Chester. *Negotiating Game.* New York: T. Y. Crowell, 1970.

———. *Give and Take.* New York: T. Y. Crowell, 1974.

Knapp, Mark L. *Nonverbal Communication in Human Interaction.* New York: Holt, Rinehart & Winston, 1972.

Kostelanetz, Richard. *Human Alternatives.* New York: Morrow, 1973.

Lamb, Warren. *Postures & Gestures.* London: Gerald Duckworth, 1965.

Meininger, Jut. *Success through T.A.* New York: Grosset & Dunlap, 1973.

Nieremberg, G. *Fundamentals of Negotiating.* New York: E.P. Dutton, 1977.

———. *The Art of Negotiating.* New York: Cornerstone Library, 1968.

Nierenberg-Calero. *Meta-Talk.* New York: Simon & Schuster, 1974.

———. *How to Read a Person Like a Book.* New York: Hawthorne Books, 1971.

Overstreet, H. A. *Influencing Human Behavior*. New York: W.W. Norton, 1953.

Poiret, Maude. *Body Talk*. New York: Award Books, 1971.

Ringer, Robert J. *Winning through Intimidation*. New York: Faucett, 1979.

Scheflen, Albert E. *Body Language & Social Order*. Englewood Cliffs, N.J.: Prentice-Hall, 1972.

Viscott, David S. *How to Make Wining Your Lifestyle*. New York: Wyden, 1973.

Articles

Cohen, Herbert A. "The Fine Art of Negotiating," *Leadership,* September 1980.

Greenburger, Francis, with Thomas Kiernan. "Creative Negotiating or Let's Make a Deal," *Flightime,* November 1978.

Harrison, Gilbert W., and Brian H. Saffer. "Negotiating at 30 Paces," *Management Review,* April 1980.

"How to Collect on Your Contracts," *The Business Owner,* November 1982.

"How to Negotiate to Get What You Want," *Association Management,* October 1979.

"How Not to Make a Deal," *The Business Owner,* January 1981.

"How You Can Get What You Want by Negotiating," *Nation's Business,* May 1981.

"The Impact of Bidding," *Consulting Engineer,* April 1979.

Kaplan, Julius. "Apres la Revolution: The Search for Creative Contract Solutions," *Worldwide Projects,* June/July 1979.

Layton, Robert. "Bizarre But True Tales from the Informal World of Arbitration, *Worldwide Projects,* August/September 1979.

Lurie, Richard, and Donald Fields. "Can Consultant Liability Be Limited?" *Worldwide Projects,* August/September 1979.

Paretsky, Sara, and Michael Silchuk. "Management: Assessing Your Liability Insurance," *Architectural Record,* January 1983.

"Protecting Your Rights in Arbitration," *Building Design & Construction,* March 1983.

Simplicus, John. "The Net Fee: Keeping the Actual Close to the Estimated," *Worldwide Projects,* April/May 1979.

———. "A Negotiator's Odyssey and the Perils of the Bargaining Table," *Worldwide Projects,* October/November 1978.

Walker, Townsend. "Foreign Exchange: What Every Contractor Should Know (But Often Doesn't)," *Worldwide Projects,* April/May 1979.

Reports

Committee on Federal Procurement of A/E Services, 1979. *Architect/Engineer Government Contracting Manual,* 1979.

Comptroller General. *Agencies Should Encourage Greater Computer Use on Federal Design Projects,* Oct. 15, 1980.

Pace, D. *Negotiation and Management of Defense Contracts,* 1970.

PSMA Management Report. *Government Audits,* Alexandria, Virginia, 1979.

Procurement Associates, Inc. *Government Prime Contracts and Subcontracts Service,* Covina, California.

Newsletters

The Art of Negotiating, vol. 2, no. 7 (April 1982).

Lines & Angles, Professional Design Insurance Corporation, vol. 1, no. 1 (March 1982).

The Professional Liability Perspective, no. 4 (April 1982).

Index